W9-AQM-584

FIELD *to* FEAST

University Press of Florida

Florida A&M University, Tallahassee • Florida Atlantic University, Boca Raton
Florida Gulf Coast University, Ft. Myers • Florida International University, Miami
Florida State University, Tallahassee • New College of Florida, Sarasota
University of Central Florida, Orlando • University of Florida, Gainesville
University of North Florida, Jacksonville • University of South Florida, Tampa
University of West Florida, Pensacola

FIELD *to* FEAST

Recipes Celebrating Florida Farmers, Chefs, and Artisans

PAM BRANDON, KATIE FARMAND, & HEATHER MCPHERSON

PHOTOGRAPHS BY GARY BOGDON

University Press of Florida

Gainesville/Tallahassee/Tampa/Boca Raton
Pensacola/Orlando/Miami/Jacksonville/Ft. Myers/Sarasota

17 16 15 14 13 12   6 5 4 3 2 1

Library of Congress Cataloging-in-Publication Data
Brandon, Pam.
Field to feast : recipes celebrating Florida farmers, chefs, and artisans / Pam Brandon,
Katie Farmand, and Heather McPherson ; photos by Gary Bogdon.
p. cm.
Includes index.
ISBN 978-0-8130-4228-2 (alk. paper)
1. Cooking, Florida. 2. Cooking, American.
I. Farmand, Katie. II. McPherson, Heather J. III. Bogdon, Gary. IV. Title.
TX715.B824 2012
641.5973 dc23
2012009807

University Press of Florida
15 Northwest 15th Street
Gainesville, FL 32611-2079
http://www.upf.com

To Florida's passionate growers and artisans, and to our husbands,
who helped us navigate thousands of miles for this book.

CONTENTS

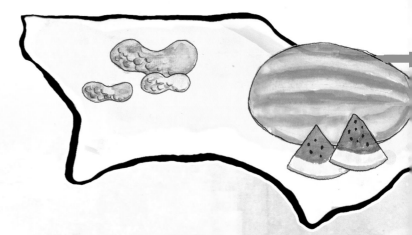

GULF of MEXICO

MORGAN CLAYTOR

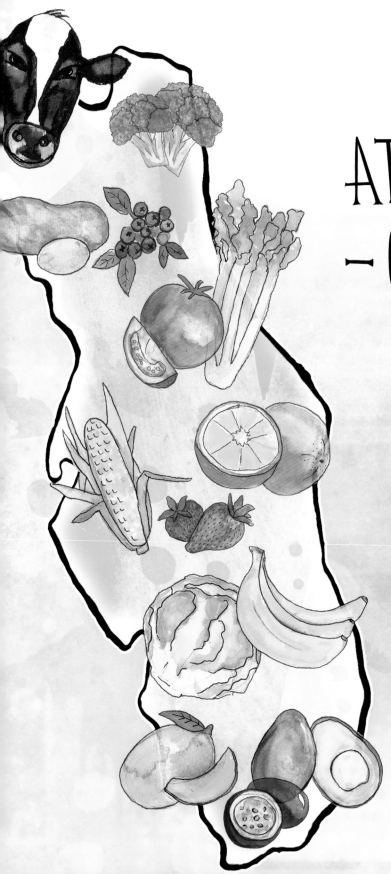

ATLANTIC

- OCEAN -

INTRODUCTION

FARMING IS BIG BUSINESS IN FLORIDA. In a state better known for miles of sandy beaches, tourism, and rockets that fly into space, our farmers feed the nation with massive crops of citrus, sugarcane, sweet corn, and tomatoes. Exotic tropical fruits that don't grow anywhere else in America thrive in South Florida's steamy climate. Immense herds of dairy cows and beef cattle graze on the flat plains in the center of the state. Watermelons, blueberries, and peanuts flourish in North Florida's kinder terrain. Nearly surrounded by water and with one of the country's biggest lakes in the middle, Florida is a peninsula of diverse agricultural abundance.

The flip side is the eat-local movement. We ask where a tomato comes from and if it's an heirloom. Is the beef grass fed, and are the berries grown without herbicides? We're paying more attention

to what we eat and how close to home food is grown—not just in restaurants, but also around the family dinner table. Farmers are reaching out with community-supported agriculture programs, or CSAs, packing up their harvest for shareholders. We're rediscovering real food and the craftspeople behind it.

This book started as a way for us to share Florida's culinary riches, and while all three of us love to cook and eat local, the breadth and depth of our state's farms simply astounded us. We split our work into three regions—north, central, and south—climbed behind the wheel, and traveled thousands of miles from the far reaches of the Panhandle to Homestead in South Florida to meet the farmers and to hear their stories. The hardest part was paring down our wish list of places to visit and people to meet.

Our curiosity propelled us on an unforgettable journey, feasting on fried duck eggs for breakfast in Bonifay, hot boiled peanuts on a front porch in Milton, juicy mangos in Lantana. We savored sugar-sweet strawberries in Plant City and heirloom tomatoes still warm from the sun in Homestead. We learned that prized tupelo honey comes from a tree which blossoms just three to four weeks each spring, and that goat-milking season is between March and September. We were captivated by farmers who have tilled the same land for generations, and neo-agrarians looking for ways to change the way the world eats.

When we asked for recipes, we were gifted with treasures from farm kitchens, such as Renee Savary's crispy roast duck, a grown-up grilled cheese from Jodi Swank, and Reda Larson's divine peanut butter pie. And we couldn't forget Florida's innovative chefs who have changed the way we eat—from last century's New World Cuisine pioneers such as Norman Van Aken and Allen Susser to a new generation that values Florida's amazing bounty and respects local growers. We're sharing their fantastic recipes, too, along with some from our own repertoires.

Comparing notes, we agreed that the one thing the farmers, artisans, and chefs share is a passion for their work and a desire to be good stewards of the earth. As one South Florida farmer said, "We're just borrowing the land from future generations." It was an honor and a privilege to shake the hands that feed us.

Our hope is that it all adds up to a delicious read and that you will be inspired to eat local and savor the diverse tastes of Florida. Let's get cooking!

SIPS & STARTERS

GABY'S FARM

HOMESTEAD

One taste of Gaby's dragon fruit sorbet is a revelation—such little fruit, such big taste. With other-worldly looks and complex flavors, dozens of exotic tropical fruits grow at Dr. Gaby Berryer's 2½-acre farm, the inspiration for Gaby's Farm Gourmet Tropical Fruit Ice Cream and Sorbet. She picks, juices, and creates the frozen treats in more than thirty flavors right on her Homestead farm.

Haitian-born Gaby was a psychologist living in North Miami with a backyard garden of tropical fruit trees when she discovered rural Homestead on a weekend excursion. "I was mesmerized," Gaby says. "I started coming back weekends and discovered this old mango grove." Today her home is a lovely tree house built above ground on steel girders in the middle of the grove.

She nurtures pomegranates, jaboticabas, canistels, macadamias, anonas, longans, lychees, mangos, sapodillas, and white and black sapotes, among others. It was the black sapote, which she calls "chocolate pudding fruit," that started her ice cream odyssey. She was awarded a grant to start the business and moved full time to the farm in 2000.

Gaby uses passion fruit to make both ice cream and sorbet, and her freshly squeezed, sweet-tart passion fruit juice is a splendid sip of the tropics.

FRESH PASSION FRUIT JUICE

"Some passion fruit is sweeter than others," Gaby says. "If you're using the small purple variety, you'll need more fruit. The larger yellow variety is more tart, but it takes less pulp to flavor the juice."

MAKES 1½ QUARTS

4 cups water, divided
1 cup sugar
2 cups passion fruit pulp, including seeds
 (about 6 passion fruits)

1 Stir together 1 cup water and the sugar in a small saucepan over medium heat. Stir until sugar dissolves. Remove the simple syrup from heat and cool to room temperature.

2 Mix passion fruit pulp and remaining water in a bowl and stir to combine; you may use a whisk or hand mixer on low speed to break the capsules around the seeds. Let mixture sit for 20 minutes at room temperature.

3 Strain pulp into a pitcher, pressing on solids to extract as much juice as possible. Discard pulp.

4 Stir simple syrup into juice and refrigerate.

4 ORANGE PREMIUM VODKA

PALM BEACH GARDENS

4 Orange Premium Vodka is, as you might guess, created from four varieties of oranges harvested from the fertile Peace River basin in the state's southwest peninsula. Made in small batches at Florida's first registered distillery, Florida Distillers Co., established in 1943 at Lake Alfred, the vodka is distilled from citrus molasses created from the juice of four distinct orange varieties—Parson Brown, Temple, Valencia, and Hamlin—known for their juiciness and bright flavor.

PEACE RIVER CAIPIROSKA

A caipiroska is a version of the Brazilian caipirinha using vodka instead of the traditional cachaça. It's a stiff drink, perfect for sipping at the end of a long day. Make simple syrup by combining 1 cup water and 1 cup sugar in a saucepan. Cook over medium heat, stirring until sugar is dissolved, then cool to room temperature.

MAKES 1 DRINK

2 slices orange
2 slices lime
1 tablespoon simple syrup
1½ ounces 4 Orange Premium Vodka
Ice
3 dashes bitters
Lime slice, for garnish

1 Place oranges, lime, and simple syrup in the bottom of a cocktail shaker. Mash with a wooden spoon or cocktail muddler. Add vodka and ice and shake to combine.

2 Pour into a double rocks glass. Sprinkle with bitters, and garnish with lime.

DRUM CIRCLE DISTILLING

SARASOTA

At Drum Circle, spirits are handcrafted in small batches using high-quality ingredients, artisanal fermentation, and copper stills. The family-run distillery produces Siesta Key White Rum and barrel-aged Siesta Key Gold Rum in a hands-on process producing small batches. Spiced rum, several infused and flavored rums, and premium vodka are in the works. The rum that started it all includes locally grown sugarcane and yeast from the French West Indies.

SIESTA KEY LIME MARTINI

This will add a kick to your next sunset party. It's reminiscent of the classic lime daiquiri—a favorite of Floridians since Hemingway's days in Key West.

MAKES 1 MARTINI

½ tablespoon superfine sugar
1½ parts Siesta Key White Rum
1 part premium orange liqueur
1½ parts fresh Key lime juice
Ice
Lime slice, for garnish

1 Dip rim of martini glass in water, then dip in sugar.

2 Combine rum, liqueur, and lime juice in a cocktail shaker with ice. Shake and strain into martini glass. Garnish with lime slice.

PARKESDALE FARMS AND MARKET

PLANT CITY

In 1956, Irish immigrant R. E. "Roy" Parke Jr. moved with his family to Florida to pursue his father's passion for farming, after learning that Plant City was the prime location for growing winter vegetables and strawberries. They formed Parkesdale Farms, and over the years, Roy and his family took on the business with zeal. They expanded the farm into hundreds of acres of strawberries, citrus, and vegetables. The Parkes also added their own plant nurseries, which hold four extensive greenhouses, where they produce over a million vegetables and flowering plants annually.

In 1969, Roy's daughter, Cheryl, and her husband, Jim Meeks, opened Parkesdale Farm Market as a small farm stand. Today the family business is spread out over 170 acres just east of Tampa in the region that is known as the Winter Strawberry Capital of the World.

SPICY STRAWBERRY MARGARITA

Adding fresh jalapeño to the plump, sweet strawberries gives this drink a tongue-tingling kick. Reduce the spiciness by removing the veins and seeds from the pepper—that's where the heat lives.

MAKES 1 DRINK

1 lime wedge
1 tablespoon brown sugar
1 teaspoon coarse salt
Ice
4 large, ripe strawberries, hulled
1 to 2 slices fresh jalapeño
¼ cup fresh orange juice
2 tablespoons fresh lime juice
3 ounces premium tequila
2 tablespoons agave nectar or simple syrup
   (To make simple syrup, stir together 1 cup
   water and 1 cup sugar in a small saucepan over
   medium heat. Stir until sugar dissolves. Remove
   the simple syrup from heat and cool to room
   temperature.)

1 Run lime wedge around edge of rocks glass. Mix brown sugar and salt on a plate and dip glass in mixture to coat rim. Fill glass with ice; set aside.

2 Muddle berries and jalapeño slices in a cocktail shaker with a muddler or back of a spoon until well mashed.

3 Add orange juice, lime juice, tequila, and agave nectar or simple syrup and fill shaker with ice. Shake vigorously, then strain mixture into prepared glass.

FAVORITE FARMS

DOVER

Marvin and Linda Brown began farming in 1976 with an acre of strawberries in Lakeland. Marvin quit his job as a machinist, and they sharecropped thirty acres with R. J. Williamson. "I just had a burning desire to farm," says Marvin. In the growing season of 1978–79, they formed Favorite Farms and leased a plot of land in Hillsborough County, where they farmed twenty-eight acres of strawberries. Eventually they bought their own land, and their first season they had sixty acres of strawberries and thirty acres of spring cherry tomatoes. Their continued success allowed them to pour their profits into the purchase of more land. Throughout the years, Linda has worked right alongside Marvin doing whatever needs to be done, from driving a tractor to managing the brokerage office.

"My father was a pioneer in using drip irrigation successfully," says Marvin's daughter, Lisa Fox. Success led to more farms and more acreage. With Ronnie Young, Marvin purchased Three Star Farms and started Sydney Farms and Strawberry Station. Eventually, Berry Bay Farms was added to the fold. It's hard to throw a strawberry in Dover without hitting something Marvin has had his hand in.

FLORIDA GARDEN SANGRIA

The main ingredients for this spirited fruity drink benefit from a long chill. During that time the fruits will exude some of their juices and the flavors will meld.

SERVES 8

2 bottles dry white wine
1¼ cups brandy
¾ cup orange liqueur
1 small orange, sliced
¼ bunch fresh mint leaves
¼ cup fresh blueberries
¼ cup fresh raspberries
1 pint strawberries, stemmed and thickly sliced
1 cup club soda, chilled
½ lemon, thinly sliced
Lime wedges, for garnish
Fresh mint, for garnish

1 In a large container, combine wine, brandy, orange liqueur, orange slices, mint, blueberries, raspberries, and strawberries. Cover and refrigerate 8 hours.

2 Before serving, add club soda and lemon slices to chilled fruit mixture. Stir to combine. Garnish serving glasses with a lime wedge and sprig of mint.

PALM RIDGE RESERVE

UMATILLA

Inside Dick and Marti Waters's converted horse barn sits an 8-foot copper behemoth that produces artisanal Florida sipping whiskey. This isn't your great-grandfather's moonshine. Palm Ridge Reserve is handcrafted 90-proof whiskey that can be found along with other top-shelf pours in bars and restaurants in Central Florida.

The strong, clear liquid is carefully funneled into small white-oak barrels to age for several months—Dick says the process smoothes the taste. He and Marti are one of only a handful of microdistillers in the state. They use Florida-grown corn, along with barley malt, toasted flaked rye, and rye malt to produce the mash for the whiskey.

Dick, a retired plumber, got into the whiskey business when he was looking for ways to earn a living and "never have to leave" the couple's sprawling ranch. "At our volume, we're probably not going to get rich," says Marti. "We don't get the price breaks on ingredients and bottles the big companies get. We're just trying to produce a good whiskey and hopefully make some money at it."

"It's a lot of work," adds Dick, looking out over the cattle slowly walking toward the fence. The setting sun has turned the pasture a plush velvet green. Dick sits on the porch steps and takes a sip of whiskey. "But I think it's worth it."

UMATILLA SMASH

Noted Winter Park bartender Larry Foor developed this cocktail to showcase the rich flavor of the artisanal whiskey. Make simple syrup by combining 1 cup water and 1 cup sugar in a saucepan and cooking until the sugar is dissolved. Cool completely before using and store leftovers in the refrigerator.

MAKES 1 DRINK

3 Florida orange wedges
4 or 5 fresh mint leaves
Splash of simple syrup
Ice
2 ounces Palm Ridge Reserve whiskey
Splash of soda water

1 Crush the oranges, mint, and simple syrup in a cocktail shaker with a muddler or the back of a spoon. Fill with ice and add whiskey.

2 Place lid on shaker and shake to combine ingredients. Pour into a glass and top with soda water.

CHEF ALLEN SUSSER

MIANI

Chef Allen Susser arrived in South Florida in the 1980s and remembers the joy of discovering the bounty of Florida's farms and waters. But it was exotic tropical fruits that held the most fascination.

"I befriended tropical fruit farmers," says Allen. "I drove to Redland, Kendall, and Homestead to meet with them and learn about the seasonality of fruits and vegetables and to find new tastes."

The quest for healthful, imaginative ingredients was the start of vibrant, multicultural cuisine in South Florida's top-tier restaurants, putting Miami on the culinary map. One of the tastemakers known as the "Mango Gang," with chefs Norman Van Aken, Mark Militello, Douglas Rodriguez, and Robbin Haas, Allen helped popularize native tropical fruits, transforming them into salads, sauces, cocktails, and more.

"It was a new way of cooking, utilizing the sweetness and acidity and richness of these fruits," Allen says. "There was real inspiration going to the farm and seeing food growing . . . a real education for me."

Today many of South Florida's top chefs embrace this pioneer's philosophy, celebrating local farms in their kitchens. And Allen still is seeking new ideas and spreading the farm-to-table gospel. "The reality is, it's not easy," says Allen. "We shouldn't stop at the restaurant, but inspire families to grow gardens, to shop at farmers' markets—be part of an ongoing symbiotic relationship."

MAHI MAHI AND LONGAN CEVICHE

Chef Allen's exceptional knowledge of tropical fruits shines in his recipes. The clean tang of the lime-laced ceviche gets a sweet counterpoint from longans, small fruit with translucent white, juicy-soft pulp that is delicately flavored.

SERVES 4

8 ounces mahi mahi, sliced into thin, 2-inch-long
  pieces
1 cup fresh lime juice
½ cup fresh orange juice
1 small sweet onion, cut into thin strips
4 large plum tomatoes, peeled, seeded, and diced
1 medium jalapeño, seeded and diced
12 medium longans, peeled and seeded, divided
2 tablespoons chopped fresh cilantro, plus 4
  sprigs
2 teaspoons coarse salt, plus additional to taste
2 tablespoons extra virgin olive oil

1 Combine mahi mahi, lime juice, and orange juice in a small stainless steel bowl, tossing to coat evenly. Cover and refrigerate for 1 hour, or until fish turns opaque, stirring occasionally.

2 Combine onion, tomatoes, jalapeño, 6 longans, and chopped cilantro in another stainless steel bowl; season mixture with 2 teaspoons coarse salt. Refrigerate.

3 Just before serving, strain almost all juice from fish. Stir fish into vegetables; season to taste with salt. Refrigerate at least 20 minutes or up to 2 hours.

4 To serve, drizzle the fish with olive oil, toss lightly, and spoon into 4 chilled martini glasses. Garnish with cilantro sprigs and remaining longans.

WHAT IS A CSA?

Community-supported agriculture programs, or CSAs, are a way to buy local, seasonal food directly from farmers. The idea was launched in the mid-1980s and continues to grow as consumers seek to know more about where their food is grown.

Farms that participate grow some or all of their produce for members or subscribers, who pay a fee up front for a portion of the harvest. It's a win for both the farmer and the member, as small farms get a dependable source of income to help pay for operations, and shareholders receive fresh produce, grass-fed beef, eggs, honey, and other farm products. Typically, once a week throughout the farming season, members have their "share" delivered, or they pick up at a drop site, with food usually packed in a box or bag.

According to Local Harvest, an online directory of small farms, farmers' markets, and other local food sources, there's no official count, but more than 4,000 CSAs are listed in its national database, and the idea continues to gain momentum as the demand for locally grown food increases.

CSAs are a fun way to try ultra-fresh produce every week that you may never have cooked before, and to celebrate the food grown near your community.

Facing: Homegrown Co-op, Orlando

VARRI GREEN FARM

OKEECHOBEE

"Our intent is to remain small and serve the local community," says Sal Varri, owner of Varri Green Farm in Okeechobee. A first-generation farmer, Sal left behind the real estate business in South Florida in 1993 for twenty acres near the shores of Lake Okeechobee. He farms October through May with a handful of volunteers and a passion for promoting good land stewardship and for producing local, sustainable, and organic food.

His crops are chemical free, and, except for a small tractor to till the land, all work is done by hand and watered from a well on the farm. About two acres are dedicated to vegetables, and seven acres are planted with fruit and nut trees. Depending on the season, you might find Asian greens, twenty varieties of lettuces, eleven kinds of beans, hot and sweet peppers, eight kinds of carrots, sprouts, herbs, and more.

"We keep it local by selling all vegetables at the farmers' market, picked a day or two before so the nutritional value is at its highest and the vegetables are as fresh as possible," Sal says. "People should meet the farmer and know where their food comes from."

Sal hosts farm-to-table dinners at the farm to benefit the local Slow Food chapter and welcomes tours, especially families and children. "It's all about community," Sal says, "teaching others what we learn, while also protecting our land."

ROASTED PEPPER BRUSCHETTA

Any combination of red, yellow, and orange peppers may be used. For a little heat, add a jalapeño or other hot pepper.

SERVES 4

5 ripe sweet peppers
4 garlic cloves, divided
2 tablespoons olive oil, plus additional for brushing bread
Coarse salt, to taste
½ (1-pound) loaf focaccia, halved horizontally
4 ounces soft fresh goat cheese, room temperature

1 Preheat broiler. Place peppers in roasting pan about 4 inches from broiler; turn until each side blackens. Remove peppers from broiler and enclose in paper bag for 10 minutes. Reserve any juice that collects in pan.

2 Peel and seed peppers; cut into ½-inch-wide strips and place in a large bowl. Add juice from roasting pan. Mince 3 garlic cloves. Add minced garlic, 2 tablespoons olive oil, and salt to peppers. Cover and let stand at room temperature.

3 Place focaccia, cut side up, on a baking sheet; brush bread with olive oil. Broil until top is golden brown, watching closely to avoid burning, about 2 minutes. Peel remaining garlic clove and cut in half. Rub cut side of hot bread with halved garlic, then cut bread crosswise into 4 equal pieces.

4 Spread goat cheese on focaccia slices and top with roasted peppers.

Sal Varri

Dale Volkert
Lake Meadow Naturals, Ocoee

HOLLAND FARMS

MILTON

At Holland Farms, rocking chairs along a shaded porch beckon visitors to sit for a while as they nibble steaming, salty boiled peanuts that were likely pulled from the ground just a few days before. Farmer Bruce Holland scoops the peanuts from giant stainless steel vats into white Styrofoam cups and happily shares with everyone who visits the farm. "If someone had said to me years ago that I'd be making my living selling boiled peanuts, I'd have called him crazy," Bruce says with a smile.

Holland Farms does indeed make most of its yearly revenue through the peanuts that grow on the farm—sold raw (green), roasted, and boiled—but the harvest throughout the year also includes watermelons, butter beans, canary melons, pink-eyed peas, and pumpkins. Everything grown here is sold here, "from the farmer's hand to the customer," says Bruce, "the old-fashioned way."

Boiling peanuts renders the shells soft and spongy, while the nuts take on an almost sweet flavor and a pleasing, tender texture. Spicy Cajun boiled peanuts are by far the most popular product sold at Holland Farms. This recipe was created—"and perfected"—by Bruce's brother.

CAJUN-STYLE BOILED PEANUTS

According to the Hollands, the peanuts only soak up the flavor of the boiling water as they cool, so they recommend cooling the peanuts completely before digging in.

MAKES 2½ POUNDS

2½ pounds green peanuts
1 small white onion, peeled and cut in half
1 green bell pepper, halved and seeded
2 tablespoons granulated garlic
1 tablespoon red pepper flakes
1 tablespoon cayenne pepper
2 to 3 jalapeño peppers, fresh or pickled
2 tablespoons rock salt
2 tablespoons spicy crab boil, such as
   Tony Chachere's or Zatarain's
1 lemon, sliced

1 Combine peanuts, onion, green pepper, granulated garlic, red pepper flakes, cayenne, jalapeños, rock salt, crab boil, and lemon in a large stockpot. Add enough cold water to cover by 3 inches. Bring to a boil, then reduce heat to a vigorous simmer.

2 Simmer for 3 hours, or until peanuts are soft. Cool completely in liquid. Rewarm before serving, if desired.

DRAGONFLY FIELDS

DEFUNIAK SPRINGS

"Our belief is that eating real food—fresh vegetables, things like that—is the best way to eat," Charles Bush says as he plucks a beetle off an arugula leaf. At his small but prolific farm, Dragonfly Fields, Charles is determined to raise food in as natural a way as possible. Aside from removing pests like the beetle, the crops are grown with a largely hands-off method. Clover and other wild plants create natural rows between the crops. Tomatoes, arugula, strawberries, squash, broccoli, onions, and a number of other vegetables are fed with the compost Charles makes on-site. "I like things in their natural, wild state," he says. "I let the vegetables ripen and grow on their own schedule."

After leaving a career in wine distribution and later as a restaurant owner, Charles now maintains the farm full time. He sells to many chefs in the area, noting that his culinary background lends itself to a relationship with the restaurants. "I love to work with these chefs," he says. "I tell them what I have, and we talk about some of the ways to best showcase the product. It's a collaboration."

PORK AND CABBAGE DUMPLINGS WITH SPICY DIPPING SAUCE

Charles's wife, Shueh-Mei Pong, was the chef at Basmati's, a popular restaurant the couple owned for years, and she still cooks daily in her role as an instructor at a high-end kitchen store in nearby Destin. These dumplings combine the Asian flavors for which Shueh-Mei is known and the Napa cabbage Charles grows. Ground chicken or turkey can be substituted for the pork. It won't have quite the same texture, but the taste will be similar. Look for round dumpling wrappers in the frozen-foods section of Asian specialty markets.

MAKES 50

DUMPLINGS

½ pound Napa cabbage (about half a small head), finely chopped
1 teaspoon coarse salt
½ pound ground pork
2 green onions, sliced
1 garlic clove, finely minced
1-inch piece ginger, peeled and finely minced
2 teaspoons soy sauce
1 teaspoon mirin (sweet rice wine)

½ cup cold water
1 tablespoon cornstarch
1 package (about 50) refrigerated round dumpling (gyoza/potsticker) wrappers

DIPPING SAUCE

¼ cup soy sauce
¼ cup rice vinegar
1 tablespoon mirin
½ to 1 teaspoon sambal oelek (hot chili paste) or sriracha (garlic-chili sauce)

MAKE AND COOK THE DUMPLINGS

1 Combine cabbage and salt in a colander and toss to combine. Set aside for 10 minutes over a bowl or in the sink, allowing excess water to seep from cabbage. Squeeze cabbage dry with hands and place in a large bowl.

2 Add ground pork, green onions, garlic, ginger, soy sauce, and mirin to cabbage. Stir until well combined.

3 Combine water and cornstarch in a small bowl and set aside.

4 Place about 1 tablespoon filling in the center of a dumpling wrapper. Dip one finger in cornstarch-water mixture and run it along edges of wrapper. Fold dumpling into a half-moon shape, using your thumbs to press out any air bubbles in filling and pressing edges tightly to seal.

5 Set finished dumpling on a baking sheet and cover with a slightly damp kitchen towel. Repeat with remaining wrappers and filling, making sure dumplings don't touch on the baking sheet.

6 Place about 2 tablespoons water in a large skillet with a tight-fitting lid; bring to a boil. Add enough dumplings to make an even layer without crowding. Cover and steam for 5 to 8 minutes, or until filling is firm and dumpling wrapper is cooked. Transfer cooked dumplings to a plate lined with paper towels. Cover loosely with aluminum foil. Repeat cooking process with remaining dumplings.

MAKE THE DIPPING SAUCE

Combine soy sauce, vinegar, mirin, and sambal oelek or sriracha. Stir to combine. Serve with dumplings.

CHEF SCOTT HUNNEL

VICTORIA & ALBERT'S, LAKE BUENA VISTA

Expectations are high at Victoria & Albert's at Disney's Grand Floridian Resort & Spa, with a James Beard Award–nominated chef in the kitchen at Central Florida's only AAA Five-Diamond restaurant (and one of only a handful in the state).

When Chef Scott Hunnel took the helm sixteen years ago, sourcing locally was more of a challenge. "Now Florida is unbelievably rich in local products," Scott says. "It's a lot easier now with more options, and the quality has improved by leaps and bounds."

Scott's menu changes daily, with a series of small courses, each as beautiful to the eye as to the palate. His commitment to adapting the menu with the seasons is clear, with kitchen standards that rival those of the finest restaurants worldwide. Much of his workday is spent on the phone with purveyors, looking for farm-fresh food packed with flavor, with deliveries arriving six days a week: "local yellowfin tuna, strawberry grouper, and shrimp out of the Gulf; pork from local farms, sweet Zellwood corn, oranges from Clermont, juicy strawberries from Plant City, the freshest eggs—there's abundance year-round, right here in our own backyard," Scott says.

And now chefs from Chicago and New York are on the lookout for Florida products, he says. "It's exciting to see what the future will bring. At the end of the day, you're only as good as your sources."

ATHENA MELON WITH GULF SHRIMP AND PROSCIUTTO

Athena melons are a cantaloupe variety that ripens early in the season and thrives in the warm climate of Central Florida. Look for melons that are heavy for their size because they tend to be the juiciest.

SERVES 8

1 Athena melon, peeled, seeded, and chopped
3 tablespoons mascarpone cheese
4 teaspoons olive oil, divided
8 large wild-caught Gulf shrimp
Coarse salt and freshly ground black pepper,
    to taste
8 slices prosciutto
1 pound red watercress

1 Puree melon in a blender. Transfer to a bowl and whisk in mascarpone. Refrigerate until ready to serve.

2 Heat 3 teaspoons olive oil in a large sauté pan over medium-high heat. Season shrimp with salt and pepper; place in sauté pan and cook, turning once, until firm and opaque, about 2 minutes per side. Remove shrimp from pan and cool completely.

3 To serve, spoon melon sauce in the center of each of 8 shallow bowls. Place 1 shrimp in the center of each bowl. Roll prosciutto into a rosette and place next to shrimp.

4 Toss watercress with remaining 1 teaspoon olive oil and season with salt and pepper. Place in bowls.

BEE HEAVEN FARM

REDLAND

"This be heaven," says Margie Pikarsky with a smile as she explains how she named Bee Heaven Farm, her five-acre spread in South Dade County's historic Redland area. Her love of the outdoors started as a child in Cuba, where her family had a hobby farm outside of Havana where they spent summers and holidays. They moved to Miami when she was eight years old, and throughout her young life she dabbled in backyard gardening. But it wasn't until 1995 that she left her full-time job to become a farmer.

Today she harvests honey, collects organic eggs, and grows fruit and vegetables, notably, her prized summertime Donnie and Hardee avocados. In 2001, she started a CSA and expanded with other local growers under the Redland Organics CSA umbrella. Margie has an unrivaled reputation in South Florida as a diligent crusader for eating local food, in season.

Summer is all about avocados and tropical fruits, and in the fall and winter she grows Asian greens and heirloom vegetables that she sells to top-tier restaurants and at farmers' markets, and packs up in weekly CSA boxes. When it's busiest, she operates her farm with "WWOOFers," or World Wide Opportunities on Organic Farms volunteers, who donate their time to working the farm each day in exchange for food and a place to stay.

MARGIE'S CHUNKY GUACAMOLE

"During its harvest season, avocado is often an appetizer, main course, side dish, and dessert," says Margie. "You can substitute lemons for limes, but never use bottled juice in this recipe. Try adding a freshly chopped tomato or cubed mango for variety."

SERVES 6 AS AN APPETIZER

2 ripe Florida avocados (1 to 1½ pounds each), any variety
½ bunch cilantro, coarsely chopped
1 medium onion, finely chopped (optional)
3 to 4 garlic cloves, crushed or finely chopped
Favorite fresh hot peppers, chopped, to taste
1 to 2 Key limes, or 1 Persian lime, juiced
Coarse sea salt and freshly ground black pepper, to taste

1 Peel and cut avocados into 1-inch chunks.

2 Stir avocados, cilantro, onion, garlic, hot peppers, and lime juice with a fork in a large bowl. Do not mash. Season to taste with salt and pepper.

CHEF HENRY SALGADO

SPANISH RIVER GRILL, NEW SMYRNA BEACH

Chef Henry Salgado thrives on seasonal menus and his interactions with local purveyors. And the results show in the long lines at his Spanish River Grill in east Volusia County. The barrier-island eatery is a dining destination for Central Floridians. Henry learned from his mentors to develop relationships with local farmers early on in his career at such prestigious locations as Hotel La Valencia in San Diego, Max's Grill in Boca Raton, and the Horseradish Grill in Atlanta.

Henry, a nominee for the 2012 James Beard Award, says the turning point in his career was working with Scott Peacock at the Horseradish Grill. "There was no looking back," he says with a laugh. "I developed a spiritual connection with the food. There was no throwing boxes of produce from the farmers' trucks into the walk-in coolers. Peacock maintained every ingredient should be respected and treated with kid gloves. I truly believe that."

Henry met his wife, Michele, while at the Horseradish Grill, and the two relocated to New Smyrna Beach to open Spanish River Grill. The menu is seasonally driven and clearly reflects his Spanish-Cuban heritage. Henry immediately cultivated relationships with local farmers. "There are farms all over this area," he says. "Most people speed by them every day without noticing. To some extent, that's good. It lets the farmers do their thing. On the other hand, there is a real void with many people about the farm-to-table connection. I try to bridge that gap by referencing my sources on menus as much as possible."

And it is not unusual to see Henry bidding at local Future Farmers of America livestock auctions. "That is a lost part of Americana," he says. "The pride in these young farmers is remarkable."

SPICY GREENS WITH ROASTED CORN AND CREAMY MANCHEGO DRESSING

This recipe leans heavily on traditional Spanish ingredients—Manchego cheese, made from sheep's milk; buttery Marcona almonds; and salty Serrano ham. You may substitute regular almonds for the Marcona and prosciutto or bacon for the Serrano.

SERVES 6 TO 8

½ cup grated Manchego cheese

½ cup sour cream

¼ cup mayonnaise

2 tablespoons buttermilk, or more as needed

2 teaspoons minced green onion, including white and light green parts

1½ teaspoons sugar

½ teaspoon Worcestershire sauce

½ teaspoon Cholula hot sauce, or your favorite hot sauce

¼ teaspoon coarse salt

¼ teaspoon freshly ground black pepper

2 teaspoons olive oil

1 cup fresh corn kernels

1 large bunch mixed bitter greens (such as arugula, dandelion greens, or mustard greens), well washed and dried

2 tablespoons chopped Marcona almonds, for garnish

2 tablespoons chopped Serrano ham, cooked until crisp, for garnish

1 Combine Manchego, sour cream, mayonnaise, buttermilk, green onion, sugar, Worcestershire sauce, hot sauce, salt, and pepper in the work bowl of a food processor and process until smooth and creamy, adding more buttermilk if necessary to achieve desired consistency. Set aside.

2 Heat olive oil in a medium sauté pan over medium-high heat. Cook corn until golden brown. Toss corn and greens with dressing to coat. Evenly divide among serving plates and garnish with almonds and crispy ham.

TERK'S ACRES

ST. AUGUSTINE

It started with a gift. When Sharon TerKeurst and her husband, Dudley, told friends they were starting a farm, people started giving them animals. "It was funny, really. We got coon hounds, donkeys, chickens, German shepherds, and a Nubian milk goat," Sharon says. "Only the goat stuck."

They moved the farm to St. Augustine twenty-five years ago and concentrated on raising milk goats full time. Sharon, who majored in nutrition in college, says she was impressed by the benefits of goat's milk versus cow's milk. "The calcium is more accessible in goat's milk," she says. She tells the story of how her mother, who had osteoporosis, drank a small glass of goat's milk every day and improved her bone density "immensely" over the course of four years.

But it's not just the nutritive value that hooked the TerKeursts on raising dairy goats and making cheese. Sharon makes cheeses—from soft crème chèvre to a mild, nutty feta—and yogurt, and sells them along with the milk itself each week at the St. Augustine Old City Farmers Market. "It's good for you," she says, "but it's also really delicious."

GOAT'S MILK PANNA COTTA WITH ARUGULA

Though most people think of panna cotta as a dessert, a savory goat's milk version is a refreshing and unexpected way to accompany a bed of fresh greens. Goat's milk and soft chèvre add a light tanginess, and spicy arugula balances the panna cotta's creamy richness.

SERVES 6

1½ teaspoons powdered unflavored gelatin
2 tablespoons cold water
1¼ cups goat's milk
1 cup whole milk
¼ cup soft goat cheese
1 tablespoon chopped fresh dill
¼ teaspoon coarse salt
¼ teaspoon freshly ground black pepper
4 cups fresh arugula
1 tablespoon red-wine vinegar
1 tablespoon extra virgin olive oil
Fresh dill, for garnish

1 Place gelatin in a bowl and sprinkle with the water. Let stand for 5 minutes.

2 Combine goat's milk, whole milk, and goat cheese in a small saucepan over medium heat. Cook, stirring, until cheese is melted and combined with milks. Stir dissolved gelatin into warm milk mixture, whisking lightly to combine. Stir in chopped dill, salt, and pepper.

3 Divide mixture among 6 (4-ounce) ramekins. Cool to room temperature and then refrigerate until cold and set.

4 Place arugula in a medium bowl and drizzle lightly with vinegar and olive oil. Toss lightly to combine. Divide arugula evenly among 6 serving plates.

5 Dip base of each ramekin in warm water for 5 seconds and then invert each panna cotta next to arugula. Garnish with fresh dill.

PINE ISLAND BOTANICALS

BOKEELIA

Fringed with mangroves and considered by many to be the last fragment of Old Florida, Pine Island remains relatively untouched by development because it has no beaches. The peaceful island is largely zoned for agriculture, with fruit tree orchards blending beautifully with long-needle pines.

Neo-agrarians Karen Glass and Michael Wallace started Pine Island Botanicals in 2003 on the north side of the island, where the temperate climate is ideal for nurturing fruits, greens, and vegetables year-round. On four acres they grow avocados, papayas, mangos, carambolas, macadamias, lychees, and citrus, along with organic vegetables—primarily salad greens, peas, beans, and tomatoes in the summer, and root vegetables in the winter.

Michael nurtures the plants with fish emulsion and local biowash with natural plant enzymes and uses "crab leftovers" from restaurants for calcium and for keeping away the nematodes. "We know where everything comes from that goes into our soil," says Karen. "Even the water is from our own well."

TOMATO-PAPAYA SALAD

Karen created this simple salad using two of the farm's crops, tomatoes and papayas. The juicy, sweet-tart papaya strikes a nice balance with the acidic tomatoes and makes a colorful small plate.

SERVES 2

1 cup chopped tomato
1 cup chopped ripe papaya
3 to 4 garlic cloves, finely chopped
¼ cup diced sweet red onion
2 tablespoons extra virgin olive oil
2 tablespoons balsamic vinegar
Coarse salt, to taste

1 Gently toss tomato, papaya, garlic, and onion in a medium bowl.

2 Drizzle with olive oil and vinegar; season to taste with salt.

3 BOYS FARM

RUSKIN

Roy's Restaurants corporate chef Kiel Lombardo, 3 Boys owner Robert Tornello, and celebrity chef Roy Yamaguchi

A self-proclaimed hippie on a mission, Robert Tornello has created an off-the-grid hydroponic farm in Ruskin, just outside of Tampa. 3 Boys Farm, which is named for his three sons, is the culmination of Robert's longtime passion for horticulture. Wind turbines, solar panels, and reclaimed water keep this operation self-sufficient and make it an ultra-efficient twenty-first-century farm.

3 Boys Farm grows arugula, radishes, broccoli rabe, cabbage, carrots, cucumbers, eggplants, collards, hot peppers, Asian greens, leeks, daikon, mustard greens, sweet corn, strawberries, and more. Robert continually cultivates relationships with top chefs as well, making 3 Boys Farm a key provider for Florida restaurants and resorts.

Robert's eco-friendly approach attracts forward-thinking culinary artisans. His techniques, such as collecting rainwater in cisterns, are traditional, but his innovative ways of utilizing the water is anything but. The reclaimed water is not only a base for hydroponic plants, but it is also integral in the farm's cooling systems, which allow the farm to produce vegetables year-round, even when temperatures outside reach sweltering levels.

His visionary practices have not gone unnoticed. In 2010, Robert won the Florida agriculture commissioner's Agricultural Environmental Leadership Award. And while he and his team have created a remarkable model for the future of hydroponic farming, Robert's vision goes beyond Florida. Robert hopes his success can help impoverished countries set up similar farming operations. In 3 Boys Farm, the pioneering legacy of Florida agriculture is alive and well.

MIXED GREENS WITH PEACHES, GRILLED ENDIVE, SEARED SHRIMP, AND POMEGRANATE-SOY VINAIGRETTE

Chef Roy Yamaguchi, known for his Hawaiian-fusion cuisine at Roy's Restaurants, adds his touch to tender baby salad greens from 3 Boys Farm. With three restaurants in the state, Roy supports Florida farms by encouraging his executive chefs to work closely with local purveyors. Chef Roy uses sliced apples, but for a Florida touch, peaches from nearby Arcadia offer sweetness to this salad.

SERVES 2

POMEGRANATE-SOY VINAIGRETTE
1 small shallot, minced
¼ cup pomegranate juice
1 tablespoon soy sauce
1 tablespoon plus 1 teaspoon red-wine vinegar
1 tablespoon walnut oil
2 tablespoons olive oil
2 teaspoons honey
1 teaspoon Dijon mustard
Coarse salt and freshly ground pepper, to taste

GRILLED ENDIVE AND SHRIMP
Olive oil, for brushing
1 head Belgian endive, cut in half lengthwise
4 jumbo wild-caught American shrimp

SALAD
5 ounces mixed salad greens (about 4 cups)
¼ cup pomegranate-soy vinaigrette
2 tablespoons candied or toasted walnuts
2 tablespoons pomegranate seeds
2 tablespoons crumbled blue cheese
1 Arcadia peach, sliced

MAKE THE VINAIGRETTE
Whisk together shallot, pomegranate juice, soy sauce, vinegar, walnut oil, olive oil, honey, Dijon, salt, and pepper in a large bowl. Set aside.

GRILL THE ENDIVE AND SHRIMP
1 Brush endive and shrimp with olive oil. Preheat an outdoor grill or grill pan to high heat.

2 Place endive on grill cut-side down and sear until it begins to wilt. Continue cooking until charred. Remove endive from grill. Add shrimp to grill and cook until firm and pink, about 2 minutes per side.

ASSEMBLE THE SALAD
1 Toss mixed greens with vinaigrette. Add walnuts, pomegranate seeds, and blue cheese and toss again.

2 Mound salad on 2 serving plates. Top with peach slices, half of endive, and 2 shrimp for each serving.

MARK'S U-PICK BLUEBERRIES

CLERMONT

To the connoisseur, not all blueberries are alike. "The average person wouldn't know—a blueberry is a blueberry—until they start tasting the different varieties," says farmer Mark McCaffrey. "Each variety has a different flavor, and some customers acquire a taste for a specific variety."

Mark's Blueberries grows more than twenty types of both Southern Highbush and Rabbiteye blueberries. During the U-pick season, on any given day, many of those varieties are available. Florida blueberries usually ripen in April, and the fields stay open through June.

Although Mark's is not an organic farm, there are no sprays or pesticides applied to the blueberries between bloom and harvest, so the fruit is ready to eat from the bush.

SUMMER FRUIT SALAD WITH FRESH MINT DRESSING

Beautiful on a buffet, the blueberries, peaches, and cantaloupe are a refreshing trio with the tender Bibb lettuce, also known as butterhead lettuce. Soft, buttery-textured Bibb leaves require gentle washing and handling.

SERVES 4

¼ to ½ cup fresh mint leaves, stems removed, minced
½ teaspoon lime zest
¼ cup fresh lime juice
2 tablespoons sugar
½ teaspoon coarse salt
¼ cup vegetable oil
1¾ cups fresh blueberries
1 large Florida peach, pitted and sliced
½ large cantaloupe, cut into bite-sized pieces
1 head Bibb lettuce, torn into bite-sized pieces, about 3 cups

1 Whisk together mint, lime zest, lime juice, sugar, and salt in a small bowl. Whisk in oil; set aside.

2 Combine blueberries, peach, and cantaloupe in a large bowl and gently toss with dressing. Refrigerate for 30 minutes.

3 To serve, place lettuce in a large bowl, top with marinated fruit and dressing, and gently toss to combine. Serve immediately.

PARADISE FARMS

HOMESTEAD

"No meat, no cigarettes" is the rule at Paradise Farms, a five-acre organic farm in Redland that integrates biodynamic principles based on the flow of energy.

"It's management by synchronicity," says Gabriele Marewski, who bought the abandoned avocado grove next door to her home in 1999 and created the farm. The layout is centered on a circle of beds that are based on sacred geometry and the ancient art of feng shui. Gabriele started with lettuce in the circle beds and expanded the planting each season. Today it's a colorful palette of microgreens, herbs, edible flowers, baby greens, heirloom tomatoes, and baby root vegetables. Honeybees and a variety of tropical fruits, including carambola, jackfruit, monstera, mango, avocado, cotton candy fruit, and bananas, also flourish on the farm.

"All weeds are pulled by hand, and planting and harvesting are done by hand—we don't even own a tractor," Gabriele says. An abundance of edible flowers are her pride, "the highest expression of the plant's energy and the highest expression of the farm," she says.

Paradise Farms sells exclusively to top chefs at high-end restaurants in the Miami area. The farm is closed to the public except for special events like dinners that showcase the culinary creations of the best chefs in Miami. "You never know the menu until you arrive," she says, "but there's no meat, and every dish features something from local farms."

PARADISE FARMS SALAD

Here's a salad inspired by a delicious version served at one of Gabriele's Dinners in Paradise. If oyster mushrooms are not available, any variety of wild mushrooms will work. Nasturtiums are easy to grow and have a sweet, spicy flavor similar to that of watercress.

SERVES 4 TO 6

¾ pound oyster mushrooms
¾ cup extra virgin olive oil, divided
¼ teaspoon salt
¼ teaspoon pepper
¼ cup fresh lemon juice
10 cups baby greens
Nasturtiums, for garnish

1 With rack in the middle, preheat oven to 425°F.

2 Toss mushrooms with 2 tablespoons oil, salt, and pepper in a medium bowl. Roast on a sheet pan, turning once, about 15 to 20 minutes, or until golden brown and tender. Remove from oven and cool to room temperature.

3 Whisk together lemon juice and remaining oil in a small bowl.

4 Gently toss mushrooms and greens in a salad bowl; add just enough dressing to lightly coat. Serve immediately, garnished with nasturtiums.

DINNER AND A ROOM AT PARADISE FARMS

There's no bathroom, running water, or air conditioning, but if you're seeking the ultimate peace and simplicity, the Zen bungalow at Paradise Farms is bliss. (And it's only a short walk to the bathroom and a solar-heated outdoor shower.)

"It's all about being in tune with nature's energy," says owner Gabriele Marewski as she encourages overnight guests to "stop, sit still, and just be."

Mornings start with a delightful breakfast of homemade granola, yogurt, fresh fruit, and juice. And the farm is a great home base for visiting local attractions such as the 37-acre Fruit & Spice Park, where you can gather fallen fruit while roaming the grounds; Knaus Berry Farm, with legendary cinnamon buns and milkshakes and a U-pick strawberry farm; Schnebly Redland's Winery, which offers daily wine tastings; and nearby Everglades National Park.

If you're lucky, Gabriele will be hosting one of her al fresco Dinners in Paradise while you're at the farm (November to May). She invites notable Miami chefs to the farm to create multicourse feasts in an outdoor kitchen, using what's growing in her fields along with other local organic products. The evening begins with wine and appetizers, then a tour of the farm before sitting down to indulge and sip more wine.

And what a pleasure to know you're just steps from the bungalow.

TEENA'S PRIDE

HOMESTEAD

Teena Borek is something of a legend in South Florida farming circles—a young mother who lost her husband to an untimely death when they both were in their twenties, then went on to raise two sons and build a successful farm so that her boys could follow in their father's footsteps. She's also a determined crusader for farmers' rights and shows up when it counts.

Born in the Canadian maritime province of Newfoundland, Teena met her husband, Michael, in the 1970s on a summer trip to Homestead. The couple married and had two sons, Steven and Michael. After her husband's death in 1980, she was left with a 500-acre farm to run.

"I wasn't a farmer," Teena says. "I had to learn to farm, and did it with the help of my family, employees, and all the farmers around me." She was constantly experimenting and learning, and over the last thirty years she has pioneered new farming technologies and worked to promote Florida agriculture. In 2004, she was named Woman of the Year in Agriculture by the Florida Department of Agriculture.

Today son Michael oversees the farm, which is now forty acres of tomatoes in the field and ten acres of hydroponic greenhouses for her twenty varieties of prized heirloom tomatoes and myriad heritage vegetables, including eggplants, carrots, beets, celery, cabbage, and microgreens and herbs. All labor in the greenhouses is done by hand, with no herbicides. (Son Steven and his wife, Amanda, have a farm in Gilchrist County.)

Teena has her own CSA and supplies top-tier restaurants throughout the United States—South Florida chefs often visit the farm to pick their own. "We welcome visitors any time to come see vegetables growing," Teena says.

HEIRLOOM TOMATO PANZANELLA

This is one of the recipes Teena shares with her CSA members. The rustic salad makes a great vegetarian lunch on its own.

SERVES 4

PANZANELLA CROUTONS

¼ cup unsalted butter

1 tablespoon minced garlic

6 cups crustless day-old bread, cut in ½-inch cubes

Sea salt and freshly ground black pepper, to taste

6 tablespoons finely grated Parmesan

TOMATO SALAD

2 pounds assorted ripe heirloom tomatoes, peeled, seeded, and cut into chunks

¼ cup minced red onion

2 teaspoons minced garlic

½ cup extra virgin olive oil

2 tablespoons fresh lemon juice

2 tablespoons chopped fresh basil leaves

1 tablespoon chopped fresh tarragon leaves
1 teaspoon sea salt
Freshly ground black pepper, to taste
2 cups trimmed arugula
Fresh Parmesan, for garnish

MAKE THE CROUTONS

1 Drain tomatoes in a colander to remove excess liquid while preparing rest of ingredients.

2 Place a large sheet pan in the oven and preheat to 375°F.

3 Melt butter in a large skillet over medium heat and cook until it foams. Add garlic and cook until fragrant, 30 seconds to 1 minute. Add bread cubes and toss to evenly coat with butter. Season with salt and pepper. Transfer bread to the preheated baking sheet. Sprinkle with cheese and toss again to melt cheese.

4 Bake, shaking the pan occasionally, about 10 minutes, until croutons are crisp and lightly colored on the outside but still soft on the inside.

MAKE THE SALAD

1 Combine tomatoes, onion, garlic, olive oil, lemon juice, basil, tarragon, salt, and pepper in a large bowl. Add croutons and toss.

2 Divide mixture among 4 plates. Top each serving with equal amount of arugula. With a vegetable peeler, shave Parmesan over the salad. Serve immediately.

WISHNATZKI FARMS

PLANT CITY

Russian immigrant Harris Wishnatzki was a fruit-and-vegetable pushcart peddler in 1920s New York City when he joined forces with Daniel Nathel, another salesman, to form a wholesale business. Harris spent winters in Florida buying produce for Wishnatzki & Nathel and was a regular at the Plant City auction. He quickly fell in love with Central Florida and moved his family south in 1929 to set up a produce-shipping operation. Daniel stayed in New York to run the wholesale side of the business.

Harris's grandson Gary began working for the company in 1974, and by 1990, he was president of Wishnatzki & Nathel. During his tenure, the firm grew steadily. In 1987, Gary began G & D Farms, to expand strawberry and vegetable acreage. In 2001, after three generations of doing business together, the Wishnatzki and Nathel families split off the Florida division, and Wishnatzki Farms was formed.

Two years later, Wishnatzki joined forces with Allen Williford to form Clear Choice Greenhouses, providing organically grown strawberries from a soil-less growing medium. The enterprise has been a platform for innovation and experimentation in new ways to grow organic strawberries. The operation began with a one-acre greenhouse, and by 2006, thirteen acres of outdoor organic strawberry production were added to help meet the demand. Gary added another 100 acres of strawberries and tomatoes that same year.

In the 2010 season, the company was Florida's largest strawberry shipper, selling and processing an astonishing thirty million pounds of strawberries from 1,200 acres—all from the humble beginnings of an immigrant pushcart peddler.

BABY GREENS WITH STRAWBERRIES AND LIME VINAIGRETTE

The citrusy tang of lime vinaigrette is a great match for the sweet strawberries. If you don't like blue cheese, you can swap it for soft goat cheese, or leave it out altogether.

SERVES 6

3 tablespoons vegetable oil
1½ tablespoons white-wine vinegar
1½ tablespoons fresh lime juice
1 tablespoon honey
½ teaspoon coarse salt
¼ teaspoon freshly ground black pepper

8 cups lightly packed baby greens
1 pint strawberries, stemmed and sliced
⅓ cup coarsely chopped red onion
6 tablespoons toasted and chopped pecans
6 tablespoons crumbled blue cheese
6 tablespoons crumbled cooked bacon

1 Whisk together oil, vinegar, lime juice, honey, salt, and pepper. Set aside.

2 Toss together baby greens, strawberries, and onion. Add vinaigrette and toss to coat. Top each serving with 1 tablespoon pecans, 1 tablespoon blue cheese, and 1 tablespoon bacon.

FAIRCHILD FARM

HOMESTEAD

Miami's Fairchild Tropical Botanic Garden is a blooming oasis that's among South Florida's most popular visitor attractions. Farther south, Fairchild Farm, Fairchild Tropical Botanic Garden's sister outpost (formerly known as Williams Grove), is a twenty-acre property in Homestead donated by Frank Williams, who gave the grove with one request: that it be used to help fruit growers in South Florida and the world.

Today the farm is the permanent home of Fairchild's Tropical Fruit Program genetic collections, including mangos, avocados, canistels, mamey sapotes, sapodillas, and other tropical fruits. "We have the most important mango collection in the world, and a heritage collection of South Florida avocados," says Noris Ledesma, curator of tropical fruit for Fairchild Farm.

Noris travels the globe, garden to garden, collecting the best of the best tropical fruit in the Americas, Africa, and Asia. "Our focus is diversity to help feed the world," she says. But she's also hands-on at the farm, working with an active children's program, classes, and internship programs and offering horticultural advice to growers. And each weekend, the farm is open to the public to sell fresh fruit smoothies and fruit from the garden's collections.

CHILLED MANGO SOUP

With about 500 mango varieties at Fairchild Farm, Noris offers this recipe and says that Carabao, Carrie, Florigon, and Bombay mango varieties make the best soup. Fragrant lemongrass is available fresh in Asian markets, produce markets, and some supermarkets. Use the white base up to where the leaves begin to branch, to flavor the soup.

SERVES 6

2 large ripe mangos, peeled, cut from the pit, and chopped
½ teaspoon fresh ginger, peeled and grated
½ tablespoon fresh lemongrass, finely minced
½ cup chicken stock
½ cup plain yogurt
2 tablespoons fresh cilantro, finely chopped, for garnish
6 large shrimp, steamed and chilled, for garnish

1 Blend mango until smooth in a blender or food processor.

2 Combine with ginger, lemongrass, and chicken stock in a large bowl; stir well. Stir in yogurt and refrigerate.

3 Before serving, garnish with cilantro and decorate edge of bowl with shrimp.

CHEF DEAN MAX

3030 OCEAN, FT. LAUDERDALE

Chef Dean Max has cooking in his genes. His grandfather was a chef in upstate New York, and his father grew up on a farm in New Jersey, then started his own farm in eastern Virginia. Dean says he remembers his own pepper patch as a kid, and enjoying the bounty of the Chesapeake Bay, cooking and fishing with his grandfather.

His family moved to Florida, and Dean headed to Florida State University as a marketing major. But a 1989 trip to Italy, with all its culinary riches, ultimately steered his career. His growing-up years on the farm and his grandfather both strongly influenced his culinary style: modern American with an emphasis on locally sourced seafood and produce. His flagship 3030 Ocean restaurant in Ft. Lauderdale opened in 2000.

"I like the relationship with the purveyor and appreciate what they are doing," says Dean. "Keeping support locally and the quality of the product are tops for me."

The more we support farmers, the better they can be, Dean says. "Work with them, tell them what you like, don't like . . . it's working together to create a superior product."

COOL GAZPACHO WITH HARISSA-GRILLED WILD-CAUGHT AMERICAN WHITE SHRIMP

Dean is a big proponent of sweet, plump American wild-caught shrimp, fished by shrimpers who travel the seas for fresh daily catches. His refreshing gazpacho is a taste of sunshine, and the grilled shrimp make it a meal. Both the soup and the shrimp can be prepared the day before serving. Lipstick peppers are pimiento-like peppers that give the harissa (a Tunisian hot sauce) sweetness. You can substitute with half of a red bell pepper.

SERVES 6

HARISSA-GRILLED SHRIMP

1 cup roasted and peeled lipstick pepper
2 tablespoons sambal oelek (hot chili paste)
2 jalapeños, seeds and membranes removed
2 cloves garlic
1 tablespoon ground cumin
1 tablespoon ground coriander
2 tablespoons lemon juice
½ cup grapeseed oil
1 tablespoon coarse salt
6 jumbo wild-caught American white shrimp

GAZPACHO

8 large vine-ripe tomatoes, quartered
1 large cucumber, seeded, peeling optional
1 red bell pepper, diced
1 green bell pepper, diced
1 jalapeño, diced
½ red onion, diced
3 cloves garlic, smashed
1 bunch basil, leaves only
1 bunch cilantro, leaves only, coarsely chopped
1 tablespoon ground cumin
2 tablespoons vinegar

{continued}

¼ cup extra virgin olive oil

¼ loaf white bread, crusts removed, diced

Coarse salt and freshly ground black pepper, to taste

5 shakes Tabasco

2 limes, juiced

Extra virgin olive oil, for serving

MAKE HARISSA AND GRILL SHRIMP

1 In a blender, puree pepper, sambal, jalapeños, garlic, cumin, coriander, and lemon juice. Slowly drizzle in oil; season with salt. Marinate shrimp in mixture for several hours in refrigerator.

2 Remove shrimp from marinade and grill 2 minutes on each side, or until just firm and pink. Dice shrimp and set aside.

MAKE THE GAZPACHO

1 Combine tomatoes, cucumber, red and green bell peppers, jalapeño, onion, garlic, basil, cilantro, cumin, vinegar, olive oil, and bread in a large bowl. Marinate for several hours in the refrigerator.

2 To serve, puree gazpacho ingredients in a blender, seasoning to taste with salt, pepper, Tabasco, and lime juice.

3 Serve in bowls with a drizzle of good olive oil and diced harissa shrimp.

WORDEN FARM

PUNTA GORDA

Husband and wife team Chris Worden and Eva Worden founded the fifty-five-acre Worden Farm in 2003. Growing organic produce in Southwest Florida, the Wordens have taught thousands of people about local organic agriculture in workshops, on farm tours, in university courses, at conferences, and during an intensive farm apprenticeship program. They have promoted agricultural development and community greening projects within the United States and internationally.

Founding members of Slow Food Southwest Florida, the Wordens met during their master's degree programs in horticulture at the University of Maryland. They have been farming together since 1998. Chris earned a doctorate in crop science from the University of Connecticut, and Eva earned a doctorate in ecosystem management from Yale University.

The farm produces more than fifty varieties of certified organic vegetables, fruits, herbs, and flowers. Sustainable, ecological techniques are used to conserve resources and protect soil and water resources, wildlife, and human health.

"If you buy directly from an organic farmer you can often get a really good deal," says Eva. "Organic is not a fad. We may call it something else in the future, but it's here to stay."

RADISH-TOP SOUP

Eva says, "We developed this soup because so many of our customers had never seen a radish with the wonderful leafy tops still attached. They kept asking us what to do with the greens, so we came up with this recipe."

SERVES 4

2 tablespoons olive oil
1 large onion, diced
2 medium potatoes, sliced
4 cups raw radish greens, well washed
4 cups water or vegetable stock
1 (14.5-ounce) can white beans, drained, or 1 cup cream (optional)
Coarse salt and freshly ground pepper, to taste
1 radish, sliced, for serving

1 Heat oil in a large saucepan over medium heat. Stir in onion and sauté until tender. Add potatoes and radish greens, stirring to coat with oil. Pour in stock and bring to a boil.

2 Reduce heat to medium-low, add beans or cream, if using, and simmer 30 minutes. Cool for 10 minutes, then carefully transfer soup to a blender. Blend until smooth.

3 Return soup to saucepan. Add salt and pepper to taste. Serve with radish slices.

CHEF DAVID GWYNN

CYPRESS RESTAURANT, TALLAHASSEE

When David Gwynn opened his restaurant in Florida's capital city eleven years ago, one of his main goals was to develop a business that would contribute to the local economy. "I've never been much of a franchise person," he says. "I believe in supporting the community, and part of that means buying ingredients from local farms as much as possible."

The food is of higher-quality when it comes from smaller farms, David says, because it's raised by people who care deeply about what they do. "One of the best parts of working with these farmers is developing a relationship and working with them to use what they grow."

From baby carrots and spicy arugula to quail and fresh grouper, David finds inspiration in the distinctive bounty of Florida's Panhandle. "We have the best of both worlds—from pines and plantations to the abundant waters of the Gulf, there's a little bit of everything available."

CREAMY WILD MUSHROOM SOUP

One of David's favorite locally grown ingredients is shiitake mushrooms, grown in carefully shaded oak logs at nearby Turkey Hill Farm. This soup is a perfect way to showcase the flavor of the earthy mushrooms. He suggests drizzling it with a bit of truffle oil or topping with a spoonful of fresh crabmeat or a handful of cornbread croutons. If you don't have the time or inclination to make mushroom stock from scratch, low-sodium vegetable or chicken stock can be substituted.

SERVES 4

WILD MUSHROOM STOCK
4 cups wild mushroom stems
1 cup roughly chopped onion
½ cup roughly chopped celery
½ cup roughly chopped carrot
6 garlic cloves
2 bay leaves
1 teaspoon dried or 2 teaspoons fresh thyme
1 teaspoon black peppercorns
¼ cup fresh parsley, leaves and stems

CREAMY WILD MUSHROOM SOUP
2 teaspoons plus 2 tablespoons unsalted butter, divided

2 stalks celery, diced
2 garlic cloves, minced
1 medium onion, diced
1 pound shiitake mushrooms, stems removed, roughly chopped (about 6 cups)
1 pound oyster mushrooms, stems removed, roughly chopped (about 6 cups)
1 teaspoon fresh thyme
1 bay leaf
½ teaspoon coarse salt, plus additional to taste
¼ teaspoon ground black pepper, plus additional to taste
1 quart wild mushroom stock
¼ cup heavy cream

MAKE THE STOCK

1 Combine mushroom stems, onion, celery, carrot, garlic, bay leaves, thyme, peppercorns, and parsley in a stockpot and add just enough water to cover. Bring to a boil, then reduce heat and simmer for 1 hour; skim foam from surface periodically.

2 Strain stock through a fine-mesh sieve into a large saucepan. Set aside.

MAKE THE SOUP

1 Heat 2 teaspoons butter in a 4-quart stockpot over medium-low heat. Add celery, garlic, and onions. Cover and cook until vegetables are softened but not brown, about 6 to 8 minutes.

2 Add mushrooms, thyme, bay leaf, ½ teaspoon salt, and ¼ teaspoon pepper to pot and stir well.

3 Cook over medium heat, stirring often, until mushrooms are cooked down and most of the liquid is gone, 20 to 30 minutes.

4 Add stock and bring to a boil. Remove pot from heat. Discard bay leaf.

5 Working in 2 batches, carefully transfer soup to a blender and puree until smooth.

6 Return soup to pot over low heat. Add cream and remaining 2 tablespoons butter. Cook until flavors are combined, about 2 minutes. Add additional salt and pepper to taste.

B&W QUALITY GROWERS

FELLSMERE

B&W Quality Growers, headquartered in Fellsmere, is the world's largest grower of watercress, with the largest organic watercress acreage in North America. Family-owned for more than 140 years, the company's agricultural history began in 1870 in New Jersey. The company grew along with the family, acquiring other growers and slowly moving into Pennsylvania, West Virginia, Tennessee, and Alabama.

In 1929, Monroe Weaver became the first watercress grower in Oviedo. And in 1996, B&W moved its world headquarters south to Fellsmere, just west of Vero Beach in Florida's coastal Indian River County. Today the company's diverse growing regions enable B&W to follow the sun and seasons to provide a year-round supply of fresh produce to supermarkets and chefs in key markets throughout the United States, Canada, and Europe.

Wild red watercress, a rare heritage variety, was discovered growing wild in tropical wetlands—its natural purplish-red hues in sharp contrast to traditional green watercress. This strikingly colorful variety, which has a more intense, peppery bite than regular arugula, is available from B&W's Florida farms only between November and April.

WATERCRESS AND MASCARPONE SOUP

Triple-cream Italian mascarpone cheese adds a velvety touch to this soup. Garnish with more mascarpone, if desired. You can adjust the consistency with more or less broth, depending on how thick you'd like the soup to be.

SERVES 4 TO 6

½ large sweet onion, diced
1 garlic clove, minced
2 tablespoons butter
4 cups chicken or vegetable broth
3 cups fresh watercress
1 cup mascarpone cheese
Coarse salt and freshly ground black pepper,
    to taste

1 Sauté onion and garlic in butter for 3 to 5 minutes in a large saucepan over medium heat. Add broth and bring to a boil. Reduce heat to medium-low. Add watercress, cover, and simmer 15 minutes.

2 Working in batches if necessary, transfer mixture to the work bowl of a food processor or blender and puree until smooth. Return to saucepan.

3 With pan over low heat, add mascarpone and stir until melted. Season to taste with salt and pepper.

LONG & SCOTT FARMS

ZELLWOOD

Hank Scott is a third-generation farmer and the lone holdout from the lucrative north Orange County vegetable farm days. Scott and his team at Long & Scott Farms work tirelessly at adapting the agricultural landscape to keep the operation thriving, and they have kept Florida sweet corn a Zellwood product to honor the long tradition of the Zellwood Sweet Corn Festival, started in 1968.

Billy Long and Hank's father, Frank, were childhood friends from Virginia. Billy persuaded Frank to join him in Florida in 1963, and the two established Long & Scott Farms on 100 acres. For the next thirty-plus years, the business expanded to 1,200 acres with sweet corn, cucumbers, red and green cabbage, and a variety of other produce.

In 1998, Billy Long retired and Frank Scott semiretired. Frank still oversees operations, but his son, Hank, manages the farm. Hank's son, Sonny, represents the fourth generation of the Scott family's farming tradition. Their cucumbers give the crunch to Claussen, Mt. Olive, and other pickle producers.

But some other projects stay closer to home. Hank's daughter, Haley, part of the family's fourth generation of land stewards, runs the farm's seasonal Scott's Country Market. Haley's goal is to turn the market into a year-round operation by sourcing additional locally grown fresh fruits and vegetables.

"Our country market is actually on a farm," Hank says. "You can see the stuff growing as you drive up. Keeping that connection with the consumer is huge."

ZELLWOOD SWEET CORN CHOWDER

Be sure to capture the sweet corn milk when you cut the kernels from the cob, and don't be quick to toss the cob out. Even cut clean, it holds flavor essence from the natural juices. Toss the cob into the soup pot for additional flavor and remove before serving.

SERVES 6

4 slices bacon, finely diced
½ cup diced onion
½ cup diced red bell pepper
2 cups sweet corn kernels cut from cob, cobs
    reserved
3 tablespoons flour
3 cups chicken or vegetable stock
1 cup medium-diced russet potatoes
1 cup heavy cream
1 tablespoon chopped fresh parsley
Coarse salt and freshly ground black pepper,
    to taste

1 Cook bacon in a large saucepan over medium-high heat until crisp. Add onion, peppers, and corn, stirring for 2 minutes. Add flour, stirring 1 minute.

2 Add stock and stir until smooth. Bring to a boil and add potatoes and corncobs. Simmer 25 to 30 minutes, or until soup reaches desired consistency.

3 Add cream and simmer 2 minutes. Season with parsley, salt, and pepper. Remove corncobs before serving.

CHEF KATHLEEN BLAKE

THE RUSTY SPOON, ORLANDO

On her menu at downtown Orlando's The Rusty Spoon, Chef Kathleen Blake refers to her local farm sources as "friends." Not business partners. Friends.

It's an important distinction for Kathleen, who has been a conscientious culinarian and eater for many years. The theme in her career is humanely handled, hormone- and antibiotic-free ingredients. Kathleen honed her skills alongside farm-fresh and clean-ingredient proponent Melissa Kelly at Primo at the JW Marriott in Orlando.

"Sourcing local ingredients not only supports the local economy; it gives guests a bite of big, natural flavors," she says. At The Rusty Spoon, she brings an artistic, rustic twist to southern fare and pub cuisine.

"It's easy to overlook where our food comes from," says Kathleen. "We are spoiled by abundant supermarkets and year-round availability of all ingredients."

Supporting fresh markets that specialize in local ingredients and putting seasonal availability in focus also is important, says Blake. "With Florida's hydroponic farmers and extended spring and fall harvests for traditional farming, that seasonal shopping list can be a lot more expansive than you might think."

TAPENADE DEVILED EGGS

Kathleen sources her eggs locally for this old-fashioned favorite with a twist, one of the most popular appetizers at The Rusty Spoon. Discarding one egg white when making the yolk filling ensures you have plenty of filling in each egg. Make sure to use organic, farm-fresh eggs—the taste will be far superior to mass-produced eggs.

MAKES 23 DEVILED EGGS

1 dozen eggs
Coarsely cracked black pepper, for serving
Extra virgin olive oil, for serving

TAPENADE

¼ cup pitted kalamata olives
¼ cup pitted green olives
¼ cup pitted oil-cured black olives
2 tablespoons capers
4 white anchovies
1 teaspoon finely chopped fresh thyme
2 teaspoons chopped fresh Italian parsley
½ teaspoon chopped fresh rosemary
1 tablespoon extra virgin olive oil
Freshly ground black pepper, to taste

AÏOLI

1 egg yolk
1½ tablespoons fresh lemon juice
¼ tablespoon chopped garlic
1 cup mild olive oil
Coarse salt, to taste

MAKE THE TAPENADE

1 Combine olives, capers, and anchovies in a food processor. Pulse until finely chopped. Alternatively, finely chop by hand.

2 Transfer to a medium bowl and fold in thyme, parsley, rosemary, and olive oil. Add black pepper to taste.

MAKE THE AÏOLI

Place egg yolk, lemon juice, and garlic in a food processor. Process until garlic is finely chopped. With processor running, slowly stream in oil in a thin, steady drizzle. Season with salt to taste.

HARD-BOIL THE EGGS AND ASSEMBLE

1 Place eggs in a large pot and cover with enough cold water to come 1 inch above eggs. Cover and bring to a boil, then remove pot from heat. Let eggs sit in hot water for 11 minutes.

2 Drain and transfer eggs to a large bowl of ice water; set aside until cool.

3 Peel eggs and cut in half lengthwise, gently separating yolks from whites; discard two egg-white halves. Pulse yolks in a food processor or mash in a bowl with a fork.

4 Fold tapenade, to taste, into yolks; add just enough aïoli, about ½ cup, to create a creamy mixture. (Refrigerate remaining aïoli and use like mayonnaise.)

5 Spoon filling into whites and garnish with cracked black pepper and a light drizzle of extra virgin olive oil.

MAINS

DOWN TO EARTH FARM

JACKSONVILLE

Just off Interstate 10, only minutes from the bustle of downtown Jacksonville, is a rural part of town that feels more than just a few miles away from the busy city center. It's in this quieter, more spread-out area that Brian Lapinski and his wife bought a piece of property in 2007 with the goal of making their own mark in the burgeoning local agriculture scene and providing "fresh, vibrant, sustainable food," says Brian. He began tilling and planting in 2008 and shortly thereafter had a flourishing vegetable farm.

The vegetables are all grown without the use of any chemicals. The beautiful array of crops includes flowering Chinese broccoli, sweet peppers, tomatoes, spinach, cantaloupes, strawberries, and more.

He hosts an intern each year from September through June, who lives at the farm with the Lapinski family and helps out with the daily routine. "Most of our interns want to start their own farms," Brian says, "so they are really interested in the day-to-day stuff that goes on."

KALE PESTO PASTA

The lacinato, or Tuscan, kale that Brian grows is among the prettiest and the tastiest of his vegetables. It makes a nontraditional base for a deep-green, nutritious pesto that's delicious tossed with pasta.

SERVES 4

1 large bunch (about ½ pound) lacinato kale, center stems discarded and leaves roughly chopped
1 tablespoon coarse salt, plus additional to taste
1 pound spaghetti
½ cup roasted, unsalted almonds
1 garlic clove
¼ cup extra virgin olive oil
¼ cup freshly grated Parmesan, plus additional for serving
Freshly ground black pepper, to taste

1 Bring a large pot of water to a boil. Fill a large bowl with ice and water; set aside.

2 Add kale and 1 tablespoon salt to boiling water and cook about 7 minutes, or until kale is tender and wilted. Remove kale with tongs (reserving cooking water) and place it in prepared ice bath. Cook spaghetti according to package directions in reserved cooking water.

3 While spaghetti cooks, remove kale from ice bath and blot dry with paper towels. Place almonds in bowl of food processor and roughly chop. Add kale and garlic and process until everything is finely chopped. With processor running, stream in oil until a thick paste forms.

4 Transfer pesto to a medium bowl and stir in Parmesan. Add salt and pepper to taste.

5 When spaghetti is cooked, reserve 1 cup cooking water and drain. Return spaghetti to pot and add pesto. Stir, coating pasta in pesto, adding cooking water if needed to create a sauce. Serve with additional Parmesan cheese.

Brian Lapinski

C&B FARMS

On the edge of the Everglades with its endless stretches of flat landscape, Devil's Garden is an incredibly wild piece of Florida where sand turns to muck and creates some of the state's richest farmland. Chuck Obern started farming here with 10 acres in 1986 and today has 2,500 acres and one of the most successful niche-farming operations in the United States tailored to the ethnic market.

About 450 acres are certified organic, with thirty-six vegetables and herbs that are rotated throughout the year to meet market demand. Eggplants, myriad peppers, Asian vegetables, arugula, squash, grape tomatoes, melons, and herbs are among his biggest crops.

"This is the dream I've had since I was a child," Chuck says. After studies in vegetable crop production at the University of Florida, he lived in Brazil and Malaysia before coming back to Florida. He spent several years doing research with everything from watermelons to root stock, learning from some of the state's best farmers. "I worked with a lot of good people all the way through," Chuck says. "Florida has a great farm community."

In 1992, he moved to Devil's Garden and began to expand his farm, where he lives today, working seven days a week with a crew that hand-picks and hand-packs all the vegetables and herbs. And two sons now work alongside their dad. "On a farm, work never ends," says Chuck, "but the American dream still can be realized."

ZUCCHINI PAPPARDELLE

Zucchini, cherry tomatoes, and basil create this easy pasta dish with pappardelle noodles that are almost the same size as the long, pastalike zucchini ribbons. To make the ribbons, use a vegetable peeler and peel off several strips from one side of the zucchini, then turn the zucchini and peel off more. Continue to turn and peel away ribbons until you get to the seeds at the center of the zucchini (discard the center).

SERVES 2

6 ounces pappardelle pasta
4 tablespoons extra virgin olive oil, divided
3 garlic cloves, thinly sliced
½ teaspoon hot pepper flakes
1 lemon, zested and juiced
1 pint cherry tomatoes, halved

1 medium zucchini, peeled with a vegetable peeler into thin ribbons
½ cup coarsely chopped fresh basil
Coarse salt and freshly ground black pepper, to taste
Freshly grated Parmesan, for serving

1 Cook pasta al dente, according to package directions; drain and toss with 2 tablespoons olive oil. Set aside and keep warm.

2 Heat remaining 2 tablespoons olive oil in a large skillet over medium heat. Add garlic, hot pepper flakes, and lemon zest. Cook 1 minute.

3 Add tomatoes and zucchini strips and cook for 1 minute. Stir in warm pasta, lemon juice, and basil. Season with salt and pepper. Serve with grated fresh Parmesan.

LITTLE RIVER MARKET GARDEN

MIAMI

Muriel Olivares

Muriel Olivares is the new generation of urban farmer, her quarter-acre Little River Market Garden tucked in a Northeast Miami neighborhood known as Little Haiti.

Muriel was born in Argentina and raised in Miami, and her "semirural, semisuburban upbringing left a wonderful, lasting impression," she says. Her love of art as a child steered her to college at the San Francisco Art Institute, where she also worked part time as a florist. After working with floral designers in San Francisco and New York, she decided that growing organic vegetables and flowers in an environmentally responsible way would be her life's calling. She fine-tuned her skills on farms in South Florida and upstate New York before returning to Miami, inspired to find a piece of land to start her own farm.

Thanks to friends, Muriel found the perfect plot just across the street from Miami's Little River and started from scratch to create a garden with dozens of different vegetables, herbs, and flowers. She runs a small CSA from November to April and sells produce and flowers at farmers' markets and to a handful of Miami restaurants. "I'd like to get better, not bigger," says Muriel. "I'm content staying small."

CALLALOO AND OKRA SUMMER QUICHE

Muriel loves cooking from the garden and also preserves, dehydrates, and freezes fruits and vegetables for the summer months when extreme heat slows production. But callaloo and okra thrive in South Florida summers. "This quiche is one of my favorites because the flavor of the vegetables is nicely complemented by the eggs, and the crust recipe is a family tradition passed down by my wonderfully healthy grandmother, Ana María," she says. Callaloo greens are the large, edible leaves of the taro root. Swiss chard, spinach, mustard greens, or turnip greens are good substitutes.

SERVES 6 TO 8

CRUST
2 cups whole-wheat flour
½ cup warm water
½ cup olive oil
½ to 1 teaspoon salt

FILLING
1 medium sweet onion, chopped
1 tablespoon extra virgin olive oil
10 medium okra pods, trimmed and chopped
   into ½-inch pieces
1 bunch callaloo leaves, coarsely chopped
Coarse salt and freshly ground black pepper,
   to taste
6 eggs

MAKE THE CRUST
Mix flour, water, oil, and salt directly in a 9-inch pie dish until a dough forms. Handle as little as possible, since separation between oil and water is what will give you a flaky crust. Use your knuckles to evenly press the dough into the dish.

MAKE THE FILLING AND BAKE THE QUICHE
1 Preheat oven to 350°F.

2 Sauté onion in 1 tablespoon olive oil in a large skillet over medium heat. Stir in okra and sauté 3 to 4 minutes, or until golden. Add callaloo and immediately remove skillet from heat; continue stirring until greens wilt. Season to taste with salt and pepper.

3 Pour vegetables into crust.

4 Beat eggs in a bowl until frothy. Pour eggs over vegetables.

5 Bake 30 to 45 minutes, or until filling is firm but not dry. Serve warm.

Fresh & Loc
here a
Long & Sco

SMITH FAMILY FARM

HASTINGS

In early-1900s Hastings, the potato was king. Frank Johns started his potato farm in 1923, and for more than eighty years, his grandson, great-grandson, and great-great-grandson have carried on the profession. Throughout the years, the 400-plus-acre farm has diversified, but one thing remains the same—four generations of the Johns-Smith family still live and work on the farm today.

To meet the growing demand for local produce and meat, Frank Johns's great-great grandson Jeb Smith started Smith Family Beef and Produce, a CSA that offers vegetables and pasture-raised, antibiotic- and hormone-free beef.

Jeb and his wife, Wendy (a former Marion County Cattleman's Sweetheart), take care of day-to-day operations of the CSA, and their children, Jared, Cady, Jeremy, and Cayla, help out around the farm, from harvesting vegetables and feeding the tilapia to tending to their flock of chickens. Jeb's brother, parents, and grandparents also live and work on the farm.

POTATO AND TATSOI PIZZA

Among the produce the Smiths grow is the classic Hastings staple, potatoes, as well as a number of Asian leafy greens. The yielding creaminess of the potatoes is a perfect foil for tatsoi, a small Asian green with a mustardlike flavor and slightly spicy bite. The two make for a nontraditional but delicious pizza topping that's surprisingly addictive. If you don't have a mandoline, use a sharp knife to cut the potatoes as thinly as possible; you should be able to see light through the slices.

SERVES 4

PIZZA DOUGH

1½ cups warm water
1 tablespoon plus 2 teaspoons extra virgin olive oil
2 teaspoons coarse salt
1 teaspoon instant yeast
½ teaspoon sugar
2¼ cups bread flour, divided

PIZZA TOPPINGS

1 cup ricotta cheese
4 cloves garlic, finely grated
¾ teaspoon coarse salt, divided
¼ teaspoon freshly ground black pepper

3 large Yukon Gold potatoes
2 cups tatsoi, roughly chopped
Extra virgin olive oil, for drizzling
Coarse salt, to taste

MAKE THE PIZZA DOUGH

1 Combine water, oil, salt, yeast, and sugar in the bowl of an electric mixer fitted with the paddle attachment. Set aside for 5 minutes, until yeast dissolves. Add 2 cups flour and mix until dough forms a ball.

2 Switch to the dough hook and knead dough for 15 minutes, until it's slightly tacky but not sticky, adding remaining ¼ cup flour if needed. Alternatively, knead by hand.

3 Transfer dough to a well-oiled bowl, turning to coat in oil. Cover bowl with damp kitchen towel. Set aside in a warm area for 2 hours, or until doubled in size.

PREPARE AND BAKE THE PIZZA

1 Place a pizza stone or large rimless baking sheet on center oven rack and preheat oven to 450°F.

2 Combine ricotta and garlic, ¼ teaspoon salt, and pepper in a small bowl; set aside.

3 Slice potatoes very thinly, using a mandoline. Place in a colander and rinse off excess starch. Toss potatoes with remaining ½ teaspoon salt and let sit 10 minutes, allowing them to release excess moisture. Pat dry with a kitchen towel and set aside.

4 Form dough into a 14-inch circle. Spread dough with ricotta mixture. Top evenly with potatoes, creating 2 layers and discarding any remaining potatoes. Lightly drizzle with olive oil. Bake 30 minutes, or until crust is golden-brown and potatoes are tender.

5 Slide oven rack out and top pizza with tatsoi. Bake 5 minutes longer, or until tatsoi is wilted.

6 Cool 5 minutes before slicing. Drizzle lightly with olive oil and season with coarse salt before serving.

SWANK SPECIALTY PRODUCE

LOXAHATCHEE

Darren Swank hails from a northeastern family of farmers and became fascinated with the idea of hydroponic farming at age fifteen after a visit to the Land Pavilion at Disney's Epcot. After moving to Florida in 1990 and seeing all the agriculture in Palm Beach County, he purchased twenty acres and launched Swank Specialty Produce in 2001, intrigued with the possibilities of large-scale hydroponics.

Now Darren, his wife, Jodi, and their three young children are part of the new generation of farmers with 200 varieties of hydroponic crops grown naturally year-round at Swank Specialty Produce in Loxahatchee. Darren hand-seeds once a week to produce a bounty of impeccable lettuces, radishes, eggplants, squash, zucchini, baby carrots, peas, kale, beans, heirloom tomatoes, basil, cilantro, dill, fennel, and watercress, as well as delicate edible flowers. Plants flourish both in shade houses and in full sun.

Swank offers a CSA, and locavores can look for Jodi at the Palm Beach Green Market. If you want a recipe, just ask. Jodi has a remarkable repertoire.

GRILLED CHEESE WITH FIG JAM AND ESCAROLE

A leader in the local Slow Food movement, Jodi, a self-proclaimed "Jewish girl from Brooklyn," embraces her new farm-to-table lifestyle. This crisp sweet-and-savory sandwich is one of her favorite recipes. Slightly bitter, crisp escarole balances the nutty fontina cheese.

SERVES 2

4 thick slices sourdough bread
2 tablespoons fig jam or fig spread
12 to 14 ounces fontina cheese, sliced
2 cups baby escarole, cut crosswise in thin strips
Coarse salt and freshly ground black pepper,
    to taste
Olive oil, for brushing

1 Spread 1 tablespoon of jam on 2 slices of bread; top each slice with half the cheese. Mound 1 cup escarole on top of cheese; season with salt and pepper. Top with a second slice of bread; brush sandwiches generously with olive oil.

2 Cook sandwiches in a large cast-iron skillet over medium-low heat, flipping once with a spatula, gently pressing once or twice. Sandwich is ready when bread is golden brown and cheese is melted.

D&D FARMS U-PICK

PALM CITY

"Families love to come pick strawberries, older folks come for the tomatoes, eggplants, peppers, turnips, broccoli, and cauliflower," says Tania Bruschi. "I think they enjoy coming to the farm, even if only for a brief visit."

There's nostalgia in picking your own produce, and D&D Farms U-Pick in Palm City welcomes visitors seven days a week to shop in their fully stocked open-air market, or to head out the back door with a bucket to pick whatever is in season.

Tania's husband, Dean, is a fourth-generation farmer (and one "D" of the "D&D"). His great-grandfather farmed in northern Italy and taught his children the business. Dean's grandfather migrated to Pennsylvania from Italy, where he began farming and raising three sons: Walt, Amerigo, and Dale. Walt continued farming in Pennsylvania, while Dean's father, Dale, and his Uncle Amerigo moved to Florida in the late 1940s and started farming in the Ft. Lauderdale area. As South Florida developed, they moved farther north and expanded into the U-pick business.

Today Dean carries on the Bruschi family U-pick tradition. "Each month brings different vegetables," Tania says. "The discovery is part of the fun for our customers."

PESTO-STUFFED EGGPLANT

Tania's meals are planned around what's fresh from the D&D fields, and she makes this dish early in the season when the young eggplants are supple and sweet. Her family considers this fork-tender eggplant comfort food and with a salad, it's dinner.

SERVES 4

PESTO
¼ cup pine nuts
2 to 6 garlic cloves, to taste
2 cups of loosely packed basil leaves
1 teaspoon coarse salt
1 teaspoon freshly ground black pepper
½ cup extra virgin olive oil

STUFFED EGGPLANT
4 small eggplants
½ cup light cream cheese, room temperature
½ cup light ricotta cheese
2 to 3 tablespoons pesto

PREPARE PESTO

Process pine nuts and garlic in the bowl of a food processor for 15 seconds. Add basil, salt, and pepper. With processor running, slowly pour olive oil through feed tube and process until pesto is pureed.

STUFF AND BAKE EGGPLANT

1 Preheat oven to 350°F. Oil a baking dish large enough to hold eggplant; set aside.

2 Cut a wedge out of each eggplant from stem to base with a sharp knife. Scoop out center of flesh with a spoon, leaving ½-inch thick shell so that it will hold its shape when baked. Discard scooped-out flesh.

3 Mix cream cheese, ricotta, and pesto in a medium bowl. Evenly divide filling among scooped-out eggplants. Place in prepared baking dish and bake for 30 minutes, or until fork tender.

CHEFS JAMES AND JULIE PETRAKIS

THE RAVENOUS PIG, WINTER PARK

Orlando natives James and Julie Petrakis share a passion for simple, straightforward, seasonal ingredients. "When the ingredients are top quality, they speak for themselves," says James, who along with Julie graduated from the Culinary Institute of America in Hyde Park, New York. "Our menus reflect comfort food that showcases locally grown food and purveyors," adds Julie.

James's favorite food to cook is fish stew with local seafood and Florida produce. Julie's favorite food changes daily: "I like simple, classic desserts such as vanilla bean crème caramel with local blueberries tossed in Florida honey."

Both chefs have been nominated for the James Beard Award and, along with other local chefs, have carried their passion for Florida farmers to the Beard House kitchen in New York.

The Ravenous Pig menus celebrate purveyors across the state—cheese, sweet corn, tomatoes, beef, pork, seafood, berries, and citrus all come from within 100 miles. An American "gastropub," The Ravenous Pig also seeks out Florida's regional microbrews and artisanal distilled spirits.

ALSATIAN TART WITH SPRING PEACH SALAD

Spring onions are those that have been harvested early, and they add a delicious sweet taste to the tart when caramelized. Caramelizing onions brings out the deep, sultry sugars of the vegetables. If cooked too long, the onions can scorch and develop a bitter flavor. If cooked in too much oil, the onions will fry and lose the pliable texture you want to achieve.

SERVES 10

CARAMELIZED ONIONS

1 to 2 large spring onion bulbs (½- to ¾-pound)
1 tablespoon extra virgin olive oil

TART

5 eggs
½ cup half-and-half
½ cup pureed raw spring onion (white bulb and very light green parts only)
½ teaspoon coarse salt
¼ teaspoon freshly ground black pepper
½ to 1 teaspoon chopped fresh thyme
9-inch prebaked tart or pie shell
4 ounces goat cheese
Extra virgin olive oil, for drizzling

SALAD

½ cup extra virgin olive oil
¼ cup champagne vinegar
Coarse salt and freshly ground black pepper, to taste
4 Florida peaches, sliced
2 cups thinly shaved fennel

CARAMELIZE THE ONIONS

1 Peel and thinly slice onion.

2 Heat olive oil in a nonstick sauté pan on medium-high heat. Add onions. When vegetables start to sizzle, stir to evenly coat with oil, 3 minutes. Turn heat to low and let simmer 30–40 minutes, stirring occasionally. Onions should be soft, evenly golden brown and measure ½ cup; set aside.

MAKE THE TART

1 Heat oven to 375ºF. Whisk together eggs, half-and-half, pureed onion, salt, pepper, and thyme; set aside.

2 Spread caramelized onions in tart shell. Pour egg mixture on top, then dollop with goat cheese. Bake 45 minutes, or until tart is golden and center is set.

3 Cool slightly before slicing.

MAKE THE SALAD AND SERVE

1 Whisk together oil and vinegar; season to taste with salt and pepper.

2 Combine the peaches and fennel in a large bowl. Drizzle with enough vinaigrette to lightly coat; season to taste with salt.

3 Serve tart with salad on the side.

TURKEY HILL FARM

TALLAHASSEE

Louise and Herman Holley bought their stretch of land just east of Tallahassee in 1999, "kind of by accident," Louise says with an enigmatic smile, "but here we are." Set among towering pine trees are acres of vegetables, from rows of deep-purple eggplants and yellow crookneck squash to flowering fig and pear trees and strawberry patches. Agroforestry, as it's called, is an integrative approach to farming that combines trees and shrubs with crops to create a diverse and sustainable landscape.

Perhaps one of the more unusual crops raised at Turkey Hill is shiitake mushrooms, grown in oak logs under a shaded canopy. But Louise's favorites are the alliums—onions, garlic, and the like. "I could grow only onions and be happy," she says.

Each day, she feeds the crew who work the land. "Lunch is the main meal," she says. When asked what a typical lunch might be, Louise is quick to answer that there really isn't one. "When greens are in season, we eat greens, and when tomatoes are in, we will eat tomatoes. What we've realized by eating from the farm is that we don't need much of a recipe to make the ingredients taste good."

QUINOA-VEGGIE BOWLS

Quinoa is a protein-packed grain that makes a willing base for any kind of in-season vegetables. Swiss chard, a mellow and delicious green, can have stalks ranging in color from milky white to bright orange and even magenta. The best part of this dish is that you can swap out ingredients depending on what's in season—just remember to include as many colors as possible.

SERVES 4

2 cups fresh black-eyed peas
1 bunch Swiss chard, stems and leaves
  separated
2 cups quinoa
1 tablespoon plus ¼ cup extra virgin olive oil,
  divided
1 small garlic clove, sliced
2 yellow squash, diced
½ teaspoon coarse salt, plus additional to taste
¼ teaspoon freshly ground black pepper, to taste
1 lime, juiced

Louise Holley in the field

1 Place black-eyed peas in a large saucepan and add enough water to cover by 2 inches. Bring to a boil, then lower heat to medium-low, cover partially, and simmer for 1 hour. Drain and set aside.

2 Chop Swiss chard stems into 1-inch pieces; cut leaves into thin strips. Set aside.

3 Rinse quinoa in a fine-mesh sieve until water runs clear. Add quinoa to a large saucepan of boiling, salted water. Cook 10 minutes, then drain through a fine-mesh sieve.

4 Fill the same saucepan with 2 inches water; bring to a boil. Set sieve with quinoa over saucepan (don't let sieve touch water). Cover with a clean kitchen towel and a lid, and steam 10 minutes, or until quinoa is dry and fluffy.

5 While quinoa cooks, heat 1 tablespoon oil in a large sauté pan over medium heat. Add garlic and cook 1 minute, until fragrant. Add Swiss chard stems and cook, stirring often, 3 minutes, or until beginning to soften. Add black-eyed peas, salt, and pepper, and cook 3 minutes more. Add Swiss chard leaves and squash, stirring to combine. Cook, stirring occasionally, 5 minutes, or until squash is softened. Reduce heat to low, and add quinoa to pan.

6 Whisk lime juice and remaining ¼ cup oil in a small bowl. Season to taste with salt and pepper. Pour into pan and stir to coat everything in dressing.

POSSUM TROT TROPICAL FRUIT NURSERY

MIAMI

"Cantankerous Chef" Robert Barnum loves to play with his tropical fruit, creating a mélange of tastes that he occasionally shares at private dinners at his Possum Trot Tropical Fruit Nursery in Redland. Cream of canistel soup, roasted jackfruit seeds, baked avocado stuffed with crab, fried green banana crab puffs, creamed spinach with carambolas . . . at dinner with Robert, you're guaranteed a tropical experience.

But he's more a mad scientist than a chef, dreaming up quirky creations to share with guests in a dining room stacked to the rafters with family heirlooms and eccentric auction finds. "Farmers are dreamers," Robert says. "As hard as we work, we have a vision that surpasses the day-to-day."

He grows dozens of certified organic tropical fruits on thirty-three acres where his family has been farming since 1945. And now Robert is the last of the Barnums in this unique corner of Redland. "We're just borrowing the land from future generations," he says.

CARAMBOLA HONEY-GLAZED CHICKEN

"All my recipes come out of my head," Robert explains when asked for a recipe. This grilled chicken is inspired by one of Robert's recipes, with a tart zing from the carambola, also known as star fruit, and sweetness from the honey.

SERVES 6 TO 8

10 cloves garlic, finely minced
2 teaspoons coarse salt
2 teaspoons freshly ground black pepper
1 cup olive oil
1 cup orange juice
1 cup pureed carambola, about 3 fruits

1 cup finely minced onion
¼ cup lemon juice
¼ cup lime juice
2 teaspoons fresh oregano
8 pieces fresh bone-in, skinless chicken (breasts, wings, thighs)
Warm honey, for basting

1 Mash garlic, salt, and pepper into a paste using a mortar and pestle. Scrape into a bowl and set aside.

2 In a saucepan, heat olive oil over medium heat until it shimmers; remove from heat and pour over garlic mix, whisking to combine. Cool to room temperature.

3 Whisk in orange juice, pureed carambola, onion, lemon juice, lime juice, and oregano. Pour over chicken and refrigerate until ready to grill (up to 3 hours in advance).

4 Remove chicken from marinade and place on preheated grill (rub a bit of oil on the grates before it gets too hot). Cook chicken 4 to 6 minutes on each side, or until juices run clear. During last few minutes, lightly baste with warm honey for a crisp glaze. Remove from grill and cover with foil. Rest chicken for about 10 minutes before serving.

UNCLE MATT'S ORGANIC

CLERMONT

Working his family's Lake County groves as a young boy, Matt McLean swore he would never follow his father, grandfather, and great-grandfather into the citrus industry. But he did just that. After graduating from the University of Florida with a degree in business administration, Matt returned to Clermont and started a juice brokerage in 1993. Two years later, opportunities in the organic market piqued his interest and, in 1999, he launched Uncle Matt's Organic.

Matt McLean

Matt's family expertise goes back four generations to his great-grandfather Angus Benjamin McLean, who learned how to grow quality citrus without the help of synthetic fertilizers, herbicides, or pesticides. His son, William Benjamin "Pappy" McLean, carried on his father's tradition, honing his growing philosophy, which advocates stewardship of the soil as the means of producing the most healthful, most nutritious crops possible. "It's not just a lifestyle," Matt says. "It's about healthy living and healthy soils. For me, it's laying the foundation for the next generation of McLeans."

Uncle Matt's juice is a blend of Hamlin and Valencia oranges, without additives, flavorings, or peel oil, things other juice companies often put in to boost flavor. The Valencia orange is Florida's most famous variety, known for its deep orange color and sweet juice, and the Hamlin was a favorite of Matt's grandfather. Today the Uncle Matt brand includes gift fruit, avocados, blueberries, an experimental peach crop, as well as six varieties of citrus juices.

GRAPEFRUIT-GRILLED JERK CHICKEN WITH ARUGULA SALAD

Grapefruit adds a subtle sweetness and a bright citrus tang that's a refreshing foil to the spicy jerk seasoning. Jerk marinades can vary, but most include a blend of hot peppers, thyme, allspice, nutmeg, and garlic.

SERVES 4

GRILLED JERK CHICKEN

4 (6-ounce) boneless chicken breasts
2 tablespoons vegetable oil
2 tablespoons lime juice
4 green onions, white and green parts, sliced
1 Scotch bonnet or habanero chile, stemmed and
  seeded, roughly chopped
1 garlic clove
1 tablespoon fresh thyme leaves
2 teaspoons peeled and minced fresh ginger
2 teaspoons packed dark brown sugar
1 teaspoon ground allspice
½ teaspoon coarse salt
½ teaspoon freshly ground black pepper
¼ teaspoon freshly ground nutmeg
1 tablespoon white vinegar
1 tablespoon dark rum (optional)

GRAPEFRUIT SAUCE

1 teaspoon olive oil
1 tablespoon minced garlic
2 cups chicken broth
2 grapefruits, juiced
1 tablespoon chopped fresh cilantro

ARUGULA SALAD

2 cups arugula
2 tablespoons extra virgin olive oil
2 grapefruits, peeled, segmented, and coarsely
  chopped
Coarse salt and freshly ground black pepper,
    to taste
16 grape tomatoes, sliced in half lengthwise
1 large papaya, peeled, seeded, and diced

MARINATE AND GRILL CHICKEN

1 Place chicken in large resealable plastic bag.

2 Combine oil, lime juice, green onions, hot pepper, garlic, thyme, ginger, brown sugar, allspice, salt, pepper, nutmeg, vinegar, and rum, if using, in a blender. Puree until smooth.

3 Pour marinade over chicken and turn and massage to coat it well. Refrigerate at least 3 hours or overnight.

4 Grill chicken about 7 to 8 minutes per side, or until cooked through.

MAKE SAUCE

1 Heat oil in a medium skillet over medium-high heat. Add garlic and cook 1 minute. Add chicken broth and grapefruit juice. Bring mixture to a boil.

2 Lower temperature to medium-low and cook until juice is reduced to syrup consistency. Stir in cilantro and set aside.

MAKE SALAD AND SERVE

1 Combine arugula, olive oil, chopped grapefruit, salt and pepper in a large bowl. Add tomatoes and papaya.

2 Place grilled chicken breasts on serving plates. Top each with salad and drizzle with grapefruit sauce.

CRAZY HART RANCH

FELLSMERE

Linda Hart grew up on a farm near Paris, Texas, where home-cured bacon, fresh eggs, and raw milk were the usual fare on the breakfast table. Her first chickens, a trio of bantams, were acquired when she was six. In 4-H, she showed rabbits and beef cattle. After high school, she pursued a career in surgical nursing and later attended Texas A&M University for preveterinary studies.

Her career brought her to Florida and a chance to return to her farming roots. "Sustainable agriculture is how I wanted to farm," Linda says, "but at the time, we didn't even have a name for it."

Today Crazy Hart Ranch produces pasture-raised poultry, including heritage-breed turkeys, using sustainable farming methods. Animals are raised humanely in a natural environment, and the result is a superior quality and taste, Linda says.

BRINED AND HERB BUTTER–BASTED TURKEY

Brining is one of the oldest methods of flavoring foods. The brine seasons meat and poultry right down to the bone and keeps it moist when cooking. If you find you need more brine, use ½ cup coarse salt and ¼ cup brown sugar for every gallon of water.

SERVES 10 TO 12

1 (14- to 15-pound) pasture-raised turkey, giblets discarded, rinsed
1 cup coarse salt
½ cup packed light brown sugar
2 tablespoons black peppercorns
3 fresh or 2 dried bay leaves
6 whole sprigs fresh thyme
3 large sprigs fresh rosemary
2 gallons cool water
4 tablespoons unsalted organic butter
2 teaspoons chopped fresh dill
1 teaspoon chopped fresh thyme
1 teaspoon chopped fresh sage
1 cup homemade or good-quality organic chicken stock

1 Place turkey in a large, deep stockpot or another large, lidded vessel that will hold it snugly. Set aside.

2 In a large saucepan, combine salt, brown sugar, peppercorns, and bay leaves. Lightly crush thyme and rosemary sprigs with your fingers, then add them to the mixture. Add water and stir until salt and sugar are dissolved.

3 Pour brine over turkey. If needed, add additional brine until turkey is completely covered. Refrigerate overnight.

4 The next morning, combine butter, dill, thyme, sage, and stock in a small saucepan over low heat. Cook, stirring, until butter is melted. Remove from heat and set aside.

5 Preheat oven to 400°F. Remove turkey from brine and rinse inside and out with cold water. Dry well with paper towels and place in a lightly oiled roasting pan.

6 Roast, uncovered, for 30 minutes. Lower oven temperature to 350°F and continue roasting turkey for 2½ hours, or until an instant-read thermometer registers 161°F when inserted into the thickest part of the thigh.

7 During the last hour of roasting, baste turkey with butter-broth mixture every 15 minutes.

8 Let turkey rest for 15 minutes before carving. Drizzle remaining butter-broth mixture over turkey before serving, if desired.

*Linda Hart with some of her
prized heritage-breed turkeys*

TWIN OAKS FARM

BONIFAY

Renee Savary

"Good morning, girls," Renee Savary calls to her flock of clucking hens. "We have visitors today. Be on your best behavior." The chickens walk along the lush green field, pecking at bright yellow flowers as Renee meanders among them. "I wanted to do a big, big farm with lots of animals," she says, "but I needed to learn first. So I started with chickens. And now . . . well, now I really love chickens."

Renee left her home country of Switzerland for the beaches of Miami twenty years ago ("for the weather, and I'm not kidding!" she says). She recognized that the food supply was nothing like that of her native country and struggled for years to find something similar. She says the day came when she realized that, to eat the way she wanted, she had to grow and raise the food herself. She purchased land in Bonifay, in the state's Panhandle, in 2008 and immediately began preparing it for USDA Organic certification, which she received in 2009.

A large pasture is dedicated to broiler chickens, laying chickens, and ducks, all of which are fed a soy-free diet. Renee also has a garden filled with traditional rows of vegetables along with tomato plants sprouting from hay bales and an intriguing spiral-shaped planter of herbs. She purposefully plans and plants everything in the plot according to biodynamics—a nature-driven growing principle—and using organic practices.

"I'm kind of a radical when it comes to food," she says with a shrug. "But really, I just want to educate people and help change the way we eat, so we can all live better, healthier lives."

RENEE'S ROAST DUCK

Renee's favorite way to prepare duck is by simply roasting it in the oven. She tells her customers that it's not so much the recipe as the method that makes for the perfect bird. Save the duck fat that isn't used in the sauce. Refrigerated, it will last a few weeks and can be used to roast potatoes or sauté vegetables.

SERVES 6 TO 8

1 cleaned, fresh duck
Coarse sea salt, to taste
1 lemon, zested

1 tablespoon olive oil
1 onion, roughly chopped
1 teaspoon Dijon mustard
½ cup dry white wine
Freshly ground black pepper, to taste

1 Preheat oven to 325ºF.

2 Rub duck with salt, lemon zest, and olive oil, then cut the skin in a crosshatched pattern without cutting into the meat. This opens the skin to let extra fat drip away and baste the duck.

3 Place duck breast side down on a rack set inside a roasting pan. Roast for 1 hour, then turn duck breast side up. Add onion to bottom of roasting pan and continue roasting until skin is crisp and meat reaches 170°F on an instant-read thermometer, about 45 minutes per pound.

4 Remove duck from oven, cover with foil, and let rest 15 minutes before carving. In the meantime, remove onions and set aside. Pour off all but a few tablespoons of duck fat. (Reserve extra fat for a later use.)

5 Place roasting pan over 2 burners on the stove. Add Dijon, wine, and salt and pepper to taste. Whisk to combine and bring to a boil. Simmer for a few minutes until thickened. Serve sauce alongside duck and onions.

ROTH FARMS

BELLE GLADE

Sugar is the most economically valuable field crop in the Sunshine State, with Palm Beach County growing about 75 percent of Florida's commercial sugarcane, according to the University of Florida's Institute of Food and Agricultural Sciences.

Behind the big numbers are small farms that are members of the Sugar Cane Growers Cooperative of Florida, harvesting, transporting, and milling the sweet crop. "My dad was one of the founders of the sugarcane co-op," says Rick Roth, a third-generation farmer.

Much has changed since his father started farming in Belle Glade in 1949. They planted sugarcane in the 1960s, but never stopped growing other crops, such as leafy vegetables, radishes, sweet corn, and beans. "Being diversified is an efficient way to farm with crop rotation," Rick explains. "The rotation breaks the cycle of insects and diseases."

While Roth Farms focuses on using its land as efficiently as possible, Rick says he also wants to raise awareness about the issues affecting farmers today and offers tours of the farm to share best practices. "We're on a mission to tell the world that with agriculture you can be part of the solution, or part of the problem," he says. "We're part of the solution."

SUGARCANE-SKEWERED SCALLOPS

If you don't want to make your own, sugarcane skewers are available in specialty stores and in the produce section of many large supermarkets. The skewers add a subtle sweetness to the buttery scallops.

SERVES 4

MARINADE
1 cup extra virgin olive oil
2 tablespoons finely minced sweet onion
1 tablespoon finely minced garlic
2 teaspoons lime zest
1 tablespoon chopped fresh mint

SCALLOPS
8 jumbo sea scallops
4 sugarcane skewers
1 tablespoon butter
1 tablespoon extra virgin olive oil
¼ cup dark rum

PREPARE THE MARINADE
Mix olive oil, onion, garlic, lime zest, and mint in a small bowl. Pour over scallops and marinate in refrigerator 2 hours.

COOK THE SCALLOPS
1 Place 2 scallops on each skewer.

2 Heat butter and olive oil in sauté pan over medium-high heat. Sear scallops, lightly brushing with rum as they cook, about 3 to 5 minutes.

MAKE YOUR OWN SUGARCANE SKEWERS

To make sugarcane skewers, wash the sugarcane stalk thoroughly. Place the cane on a cutting board and position a sharp knife (a cleaver works well) horizontally across the cane. Be careful; the cane is harder than you might think. Apply as much pressure as you can or tap the knife with a rubber mallet or hammer to help push it through.

Trim the ends of the sugarcane and cut the stalk crosswise into 5-inch sections. Trim the tough skin off the cane. With a heavy chef's knife or cleaver, cut the cane into flat ¼-inch-thick strips. Cut each strip lengthwise into sections. Sharpen the ends of the skewers into points.

CHEF HARI PULAPAKA

CRESS RESTAURANT, DELAND

Chef Hari Pulapaka's résumé is remarkable: executive chef; a leader in the sustainable-foods movement in Volusia County; and last, but certainly not least, an associate professor of mathematics at Stetson University. Unable to deny his passion for the culinary arts, he decided to augment his culinary experiences at Canoe Restaurant in Toronto and Denali Princess Wilderness Lodge in Alaska with formal training at Le Cordon Bleu College of Culinary Arts in Orlando.

After graduating, and while still teaching at Stetson, he cooked as a private chef in DeLand and the surrounding areas as well as a guest chef at the previous occupant of Cress's space, Le Jardin Café. He and his wife and business partner, Dr. Jenneffer Pulapaka, a physician, opened Cress in 2008. Three years later he was nominated for a James Beard Award.

From the get-go, Hari, who grew up in Mumbai, India, sought out local ingredients for his menus and continues to support the eat-local movement in Volusia County, including efforts on the Stetson campus. With a passion for bold, vibrant flavors, his favorite foods to cook are anything from the Mediterranean, Southeast Asia, or the Caribbean. "The James Beard nomination and the success that Cress has slowly built is a confirmation of our efforts to bring locally sourced and globally inspired cuisine to Central Florida," Hari says.

Indeed, one of the first things Hari did after opening Cress was to establish the Cress Garden at nearby Planted Earth Vegetables, a community-based organic garden run by Nize Nylen. "You can't just talk about it, you have to be a part of the sustainable-food effort," adds Hari. "For a chef that's where the flavor begins. That's where the consumer connects back to the land." For this mathematics professor, it's the perfect culinary equation.

{continued}

GRILLED WAHOO AND SHRIMP WITH CREOLE VEGETABLES AND SHIITAKE-THYME GRITS

Wahoo is a flaky and moist fish. Cobia, red snapper, mahimahi, or grouper can be used in this recipe as well. The cooking time and amount of liquid you will need for the grits will vary depending on their coarseness.

SERVES 4

GRILLED WAHOO AND SHRIMP

4 (6-ounce) wahoo fillets

12 large wild-caught American shrimp, peeled and deveined

3 tablespoons extra virgin olive oil

1 tablespoon low-sodium Creole spice blend, or to taste

1 tablespoon minced garlic

Coarse salt and freshly ground black pepper, to taste

CREOLE VEGETABLES

2 tablespoons extra virgin olive oil

1 cup diced Spanish onion

1 cup diced celery

½ cup diced red bell pepper

½ cup diced green bell pepper

Coarse salt, to taste

Freshly ground black pepper, to taste

1 cup diced andouille or Cajun sausage

1 dry or 3 fresh bay leaves

1 cup fresh corn kernels

1 cup fresh lima beans

1 tablespoon minced fresh thyme

1 tablespoon minced fresh rosemary

1 tablespoon minced garlic

2 cups diced ripe tomatoes

2 cups low-sodium vegetable or chicken stock

½ cup heavy cream

2 tablespoons minced fresh parsley

SHIITAKE-THYME GRITS

4 tablespoons unsalted butter

1 medium Spanish onion, finely diced

1 dry or 3 fresh bay leaves

½ cup thinly sliced shiitake mushrooms

1 tablespoon minced fresh thyme

Coarse salt and freshly ground black pepper, to taste

½ cup heavy cream, or more as needed

1½ cups water, or more as needed

½ cup yellow corn grits

Sweet potato chips, for garnish

Chopped fresh parsley, for garnish

MARINATE THE FISH AND SHRIMP

Place wahoo and shrimp in a shallow bowl. Drizzle with oil, rubbing to coat. Sprinkle with Creole spice blend and garlic, rubbing to coat. Refrigerate, covered, for 1 hour.

MAKE THE VEGETABLES

1 Heat oil in a large sauté pan over medium heat. Add onion, celery, and red and green peppers and cook 5 minutes, or until onion and celery are translucent. Season lightly with salt and pepper.

2 Add sausage and sauté 2 to 3 minutes. Add bay leaves, corn, and lima beans and cook 1 minute. Stir in thyme, rosemary, and garlic and cook 30 seconds. Add tomatoes and let mixture simmer for about 2 minutes. Add stock and season with additional salt and pepper to taste.

3 Simmer, stirring periodically, about 30 minutes. Add heavy cream and fresh parsley just before serving.

PREPARE THE GRITS

1 Melt butter in a large saucepan over medium heat. Add onions, bay leaves, mushrooms, and thyme and cook until onions turn golden brown. Season lightly with salt and pepper. Add cream and water.

2 When water and cream come to a simmer, slowly whisk in grits. Stir for 1 to 2 minutes, or until mixture is smooth. Reduce heat to medium-low. Cook grits, stirring occasionally, 30 to 40 minutes, or until thick and creamy.

GRILL THE WAHOO AND SHRIMP AND ASSEMBLE THE DISH

1 Season wahoo and shrimp with salt and pepper. Grill shrimp 2 to 3 minutes, turning once. Grill wahoo, turning once, about 5 to 6 minutes, depending on the thickness of the fillet.

2 For each serving, spoon about ½ cup cooked grits in a bowl. Top with grilled wahoo and shrimp. Ladle Creole vegetables evenly among servings. Garnish plates with sweet potato chips and parsley.

CHEF JIM SHIRLEY

PENSACOLA

Chef Jim Shirley, the son of a U.S. Navy pilot, moved with his family all over the world and experienced a variety of cuisines and cultures at a young age. But when it came time to open his own restaurant, he went back to his roots—his grandmother's traditional southern cooking. He is co-owner and chef of three Pensacola restaurants—the Fish House, the Fish House Deck Bar, and Atlas Oyster House—as well as the Great Southern Café in Seaside. His latest endeavor, also in Seaside, is a food truck called The Meltdown on 30A, which turns out grilled-cheese sandwiches, from traditional to gourmet.

Jim uses his passion for native southern staples, knowledge of the local waters, and his family's farming history to promote what he calls "new ruralism," a movement to promote sustainable agriculture. He sources many of the classic southern ingredients he uses—from fresh pink-eyed peas and collard greens to oysters and blue crab—from Panhandle farms and local fisheries.

PAN-FRIED TRIGGERFISH WITH FRIED GREEN TOMATOES AND YELLOW TOMATO SALSA

"The long, hot summer days are a sure sign that local tomatoes are ripening," Jim says. "I get mine from Joe Cunningham—we call him Tomato Joe." Jim's combination of flaky, sweet triggerfish and fresh, plump tomatoes makes for a heavenly summertime dish. If you can't find fresh triggerfish, substitute with fresh snapper. Chef Jim recommends using a cast-iron skillet for true southern authenticity.

SERVES 2

BACON–BLUE CHEESE VINAIGRETTE

½ pound bacon

½ cup crumbled blue cheese

½ cup plus 2 tablespoons extra virgin olive oil

¼ cup plus 2 tablespoons apple cider vinegar

2 cloves garlic, minced

1 small shallot, minced

1 teaspoon coarse salt

½ teaspoon freshly ground black pepper

½ tablespoon chopped fresh parsley

YELLOW TOMATO SALSA

1 vine-ripened yellow tomato, diced

1 vine-ripened red tomato, diced

1 medium sweet onion, diced

Coarse salt and freshly ground black pepper, to taste

PAN-FRIED TRIGGERFISH AND FRIED GREEN TOMATOES

1 cup all-purpose flour

1 teaspoon coarse salt

1 teaspoon ground white pepper

1 tablespoon onion powder

1 tablespoon garlic powder

1 large green tomato, sliced into ½-inch-thick rounds

2 (6-ounce) triggerfish fillets

2 handfuls mesclun greens, for serving

PREPARE THE VINAIGRETTE

1 Cook bacon in a large skillet over medium heat until crisp. Reserve rendered bacon fat. Drain bacon on paper towels; chop.

2 Combine bacon, blue cheese, 2 tablespoons reserved bacon fat, oil, vinegar, garlic, shallot, salt, pepper, and parsley in a quart jar. Tightly screw on lid, shake vigorously, and set aside.

MAKE THE SALSA

Combine yellow tomatoes, red tomatoes, and onion in a medium bowl. Add just enough bacon–blue cheese vinaigrette to coat. Add salt and pepper to taste. Stir gently and set aside.

FRY THE TRIGGERFISH AND TOMATOES

1 Heat remaining bacon fat in same skillet over medium-high heat.

2 Combine flour, salt, white pepper, onion powder, and garlic powder in a large, shallow dish, stirring with a fork to combine.

3 Dredge green tomato slices and triggerfish fillets in seasoned flour. Working in batches, fry tomatoes and then fish about 3 minutes per side, or until golden brown.

4 Place a handful of mesclun greens on a large plate and drizzle lightly with vinaigrette. Lay triggerfish over greens and top with fried green tomato slices. Drizzle with salsa.

CHEF KEVIN FONZO

K RESTAURANT, ORLANDO

FL

If Chef Kevin Fonzo isn't in the kitchen of his Orlando restaurant, he's likely in the garden just outside the back door. Every K Restaurant menu begins with the best-quality ingredients he can get from many local farms, but he also tends his own supply of fresh vegetables for inspiration.

But the James Beard Award nominee has other menus in mind as he selects herbs and produce for the day's fare. Educating young children about the importance of eating nutritious meals is also part of Kevin's farm-to-table vision. At K he specializes in porcini-dusted fillets and modern twists on southern classics. But during the school year, Kevin volunteers as the cafeteria chef at a small Orange County school. When most chefs of his stature are enjoying a little rest and relaxation, Kevin is using some of his free time to prepare healthful lunches for schoolchildren and subtly expand their appreciation for a variety of fruits and vegetables.

He affectionately calls them "his kids," and he is just as passionate about their food as he is about the daily menus at his casual-upscale restaurant, located in the College Park neighborhood. Kevin involves the children in the gardening process to help them understand that vegetables don't just come from the supermarket. "A chef's role is not only to cook, but to teach," says Kevin. "It's amazing what foods kids will try when they have a hand in growing them. When they grew beets, all of the students had to have their hands on the bowl when they presented the vegetables to me. Beets. Do you know how many parents can't get their kids to eat beets, or radishes? These kids couldn't wait because they were part of the process."

SAUTÉED FLORIDA SNAPPER WITH SUCCOTASH AND LEMON THYME BUTTER

Chef Kevin says any locally caught white fish will work in place of the snapper, including cobia, flounder, or grouper. If you prefer shellfish, substitute scallops or shrimp. Use whatever fresh beans you can find—check farmers' markets in the spring for baby limas, black-eyed peas, even fresh garbanzo beans. Lemon thyme is a variety of thyme that has a distinct lemon flavor. If you can find only regular thyme, add ¼ teaspoon fresh lemon zest to the butter mixture.

SERVES 4

LEMON THYME BUTTER

8 tablespoons unsalted butter, at room temperature
1 teaspoon finely chopped fresh lemon thyme
1 teaspoon chopped fresh parsley
¼ teaspoon coarse salt
Pinch freshly ground black pepper

SUCCOTASH

1 tablespoon olive oil
1 tablespoon unsalted butter
1 tablespoon diced shallot or red onion
3 cups fresh sweet corn kernels
1 cup fresh beans, such as limas or pink-eyed peas
½ cup chopped ripe tomato
1 tablespoon chopped fresh parsley
1 tablespoon chopped fresh chives
Coarse salt and freshly ground black pepper, to taste

SNAPPER

4 (7- to 8-ounce) snapper fillets
¼ teaspoon coarse salt
¼ teaspoon freshly ground black pepper
2 tablespoons vegetable oil
2 tablespoons butter

PREPARE THE LEMON THYME BUTTER

Combine butter, lemon thyme, parsley, salt, and pepper. Set aside.

MAKE THE SUCCOTASH

1 Heat oil and butter in a medium sauté pan over medium heat until golden-brown. Add shallots or onion and cook until tender, about 2 minutes.

2 Add corn and sauté 2 minutes. Add beans and sauté 1 minute. Add tomato, parsley, and chives, stirring to combine. Cook until mixture is hot. Add salt and pepper to taste. Turn heat to low to keep warm.

COOK THE SNAPPER

1 Preheat oven to 350°F.

2 Sprinkle snapper with salt and pepper. Heat oil and butter in large ovenproof sauté pan over medium-high heat until butter turns golden brown. Reduce heat to medium and place fish in pan. Sauté 1 to 2 minutes per side, until fish is golden brown.

3 Place pan in oven and bake 10 minutes.

4 Place 1 tablespoon lemon thyme butter on each fish fillet and return pan to oven for a few seconds to melt butter. Place 1 cup warm succotash on plate. Top with sautéed snapper.

FLORIDA BEEF INDUSTRY

STILL HOME ON THE RANGE AND THRIVING

When the Spanish claimed this land and brought horses, cattle, and cowboy culture to Florida, they set the groundwork for the nation's entire beef industry. Today Florida's cattle industry is one of the fifteen largest in the United States, according to the Florida Cattlemen's Association.

Early American cattle originated in Europe, but came to the Americas through various routes. By the time cattle reached Texas and California from Mexico in the 1500s, Florida's cattle industry was already emerging, according to research by the College of Education at the University of South Florida. Despite the harshness of the hammocks, Florida's lush pastureland and Spanish explorers turned Florida into America's oldest cattle-raising state. Before 1700, there were ranches in the Florida Panhandle and along the St. Johns River, and by the 1800s, the Seminole nation had extensive herds of cattle.

Florida ranchers raise the third-largest number of cattle of any state east of the Mississippi, according to the Florida Department of Agriculture and Consumer Services Division of Animal Industry. Their herds represent centuries of enduring pioneer spirit. State research shows that nearly half of all Florida agricultural land is involved in cattle production, including four million acres of pastureland and one million acres of grazed woodland.

BEEF STIR-FRY WITH TANGERINE SAUCE

Once the ingredients are assembled, this is an easy weeknight meal. Pair with rice seasoned with a hint of sesame oil.

SERVES 4

12 ounces lean beef, such as round steak or flank steak

2 tangerines

3 tablespoons sherry

2 tablespoons soy sauce

1 tablespoon hoisin sauce (sweet Asian sauce)

2 cloves garlic, minced

2 tablespoons peanut oil

1 teaspoon fresh ginger, peeled and minced

2 carrots, cut on diagonal into ½-inch pieces

2 shallots, chopped

1 Slice beef into very thin strips. Refrigerate until ready to use.

2 Shave colored layer off the peel of one of the tangerines with a vegetable peeler, being careful not to capture the white pith. Slice shaved peel into thin strips. Peel and section tangerines, remove seeds, and set aside.

3 Combine strips of tangerine peel, sherry, soy sauce, hoisin sauce, and garlic in medium bowl. Set aside.

4 Heat oil in wok or large skillet over medium-high heat until it shimmers. Add beef and stir constantly until each piece is cooked, about 5 minutes. Remove beef from wok, allowing excess oil to drip back into pan. Add ginger and carrots to wok. Cook, stirring constantly, 2 minutes. Add shallots and cook 2 minutes. Return beef to wok. Add tangerine sections and hoisin mixture. Bring to a boil, stirring constantly, 1 minute, or until heated through and well combined.

LIGHTSEY CATTLE CO.

LAKE WALES

For twelve generations, the name Lightsey has been associated with cattle ranching. Since the 1850s in Central Florida, there have been six generations who have worked the land. Marcia and her husband, Cary, along with Cary's brother Layne and his wife, Charlotte, manage more than 6,000 head of cattle on more than 32,000 acres in three Florida counties. The seventh and eighth generations are now learning the trade.

Stewardship of the land is an important part of the Lightsey Cattle Co. mission. "One day you realize that as ranchers you have the same goals as environmental activists," says Marcia Lightsey. "Clean water, good soil, and clean air are critical to our livestock and preservation of our land. Instead of pushing back, we opened our doors and invited people in to see how our practices—such as rotational cattle grazing to prevent erosion, water recycling in our groves, and controlled burning to rejuvenate the land and wildlife habitats—have paid off.

"Our ranches are home to many rare and endangered species. We have about fourteen active bald eagles' nests, scrub jays, gopher tortoises, and black bears. Our 3,000-acre ranch on Brahma Island in Lake Kissimmee is home to twenty-eight protected species, including snail kites.

"For a Lightsey, it's as much about family as it is about ranching. We have a responsibility to preserve our land for our grandchildren. Balancing growth while maintaining Florida's rich agricultural heritage is so important."

SAUCY BEEF TACOS

This is a cowboy favorite. Add a jalapeño to the mix if you like it hot—the spiciness can also be adjusted with hot sauce served at the table.

SERVES 6

1 tablespoon vegetable oil
2 pounds flank steak, cut into large chunks
3 large cloves garlic, minced
1 large onion, cut into half-moon slices
½ tablespoon chili powder
2 teaspoons cumin
2 big pinches coarse salt, divided
8-ounce can tomato sauce
½ cup dark Mexican beer (such as Dos Equis amber)

½ cup beef broth
¼ cup chopped fresh cilantro
Corn tortillas, warmed
Chopped raw onion, for topping
Crumbled cotija cheese, for topping
Sour cream, for topping
Sliced avocado, for topping
Shredded lettuce, for topping
Lime wedges, for serving

1 Heat oil in a large pot over medium-high heat. Add beef, searing until brown, about 4 minutes per side. Working in batches to avoid crowding the pan, add garlic, onion, chili powder, cumin, and a generous pinch of salt and stir to combine. Cook, stirring often, 2 minutes.

2 Add tomato sauce, beer, and beef broth. Stir to combine. Reduce heat to medium-low and simmer, covered, 1 hour, then uncover and simmer another hour, until beef is very tender.

3 Shred beef in sauce using 2 forks. Taste and add a second pinch of salt, if desired. Stir in cilantro.

4 Spoon beef mixture into warmed corn tortillas. Serve with toppings.

PETTEWAY CITRUS & CATTLE

ZOLFO SPRINGS

Roy and Wendy Petteway make their home in the heart of the family ranch amid citrus groves and registered Angus cattle in small-town Zolfo Springs. The Petteways have raised citrus and cattle in Hardee County for generations, diversifying the farm business with grove caretaking, citrus tree removal, and a certified citrus nursery. "This was my father's house," says Roy, taking a break from the morning chores. "Growing up on a ranch is a hard life, but it's a good life. It has been for my family."

The Petteways manage their ranch with Australian shepherd dogs and a small fleet of all-terrain vehicles. "Day to day, it's less expensive than tending and feeding horses and maintaining barns," says Roy. "We hire cowboys to work with us as we need them, but this works for us."

Roy, Jr., has returned to the ranch with a degree in veterinary science. He left for school with more knowledge than most of his fellow students, and now he is working with his parents to keep their herd fit and profitable. "Our focus turned to registered Angus when we needed bulls with the genetics that would work in our southern environment," he says. "Having purchased bulls from out of state, we found that they couldn't stand up to our environment and just melted. Our program is forage based, and our cattle must work for us, not us work for them." The same goes for the cattle the family shows in agricultural competitions: "We expect them to work on the ranch afterwards."

The Petteway ranch also sells calves to 4-H and Future Farmers of America students for livestock projects and has produced several class champions and a few grand and reserve champions.

RANCH HAND HAMBURGER CASSEROLE

"When my mother died, my father had to do everything," Roy says. "This dish was a ranch staple. It was something he could put in the oven, then get back to ranching, and have a meal on the table for us. We still make it to this day." This version is inspired by the Petteway recipe.

SERVES 8 TO 10

1 pound ground beef
1¼ teaspoons coarse salt, divided
½ teaspoon freshly ground black pepper, divided
1 cup heavy cream
½ cup whole or 2% milk
1 egg
4 to 5 Yukon Gold potatoes, sliced very thinly
1½ cups sliced crimini mushrooms
1 large sweet yellow onion, sliced very thinly
8-ounce block sharp cheddar cheese, shredded

1 Preheat oven to 350°F. Brown ground beef in a large skillet; strain and discard excess fat. Season with ¼ teaspoon salt and ¼ teaspoon pepper.

2 Whisk cream, milk, and egg in a large bowl until slightly thickened. Whisk in ¼ teaspoon salt until it dissolves. Set aside.

3 Place browned beef in the bottom of a Dutch oven. Top with sliced potatoes and sprinkle with ½ teaspoon salt and ¼ teaspoon pepper. Pour half of milk mixture over potatoes.

4 Top with mushrooms; sprinkle with ¼ teaspoon salt. Arrange sliced onion and cheese on top. Pour remaining milk mixture over top.

5 Bake, uncovered, for 1½ to 2 hours, or until potatoes are soft and onions are tender.

GREEN CEDARS FARM

MOLINO

Roger Elliot has the calm, patient demeanor of a true southern gentleman, which comes in handy when he's leading groups of sixty or so third-graders around his farm, a weekly occurrence here. "Some things, you just can't teach in the classroom," Roger says. "You have to see them firsthand. So it's great to see the kids realize that this is where chickens, or eggs, or carrots come from."

He knows the importance of education in agriculture after spending part of his career as a University of Florida Institute of Food and Agricultural Sciences extension livestock and small farms agent (before that, he was a navy helicopter pilot). Today he and his wife, Pam, raise lambs, sheep, pastured poultry, and eggs and tend a modest-sized apple orchard and a small but prolific vegetable garden.

Green Cedars Farm looks like the stuff of storybooks: a barn filled with peeping chicks, friendly horses, and a crowing rooster. Outside, the bleating sheep wander closer to greet visitors while the hens cluck and gather around their solar-powered laying house. Perhaps the most enchanting of the residents are the pair of peacocks that still cling to their "mother"—a chicken that was given the job of keeping them warm as babies, and has still never left their side.

Many of the livestock Roger raises are heritage breeds, something he says is important for the future of small farms and a healthful food supply. The lamb they raise, Pam says, is mild in flavor, and the thinner cuts are perfect for quick cooking like a steak. For the less tender cuts, the Elliots stick to a low-and-slow method, as for this simple stew, which includes green, leafy kale and fresh butter beans for a comforting one-pot meal.

LAMB AND KALE STEW

If you want to use boneless stew meat, substitute low-sodium chicken or beef broth for half of the water and taste before adding the remaining salt. Speckled butter beans are essentially the same as their cream-colored counterparts, just with a pink-brown hue. Fresh lima beans may be substituted.

SERVES 4 TO 6

1½ pounds bone-in lamb stew meat
1 large onion, diced
8 cups water
1 teaspoon coarse salt, divided
2 cups fresh speckled butter beans
2 large bunches fresh kale, stems removed, leaves
   chopped (about 4 cups)
4 cloves garlic, minced
2 potatoes, diced
½ teaspoon ground black pepper

1 Combine lamb and onion in large stockpot. Cover with water and bring to a boil. Add ½ teaspoon salt. Lower heat to medium-low, cover pot, and simmer until meat is tender, about 1 hour.

2 Add butter beans, kale, garlic, potatoes, remaining ½ teaspoon salt, and pepper to pot, stirring to combine. Simmer, stirring occasionally, until meat is falling apart and vegetables are very tender.

DEEP CREEK RANCH

DELEON SPRINGS

Designated a Century Pioneer Family Farm by the Florida Department of Agriculture and Consumer Services, Deep Creek Ranch easily could have maintained the status quo, built on the past, and added a few modern farming techniques. Instead, Deep Creek is among the growing number of farms that are plotting a new course for Florida's next 100 years.

Active supporters of the Slow Food movement, the Strawns have shifted the focus of their family ranch to producing superior grass-fed or grain-supplemented beef and lamb. Deep Creek sells to consumers at Central Florida farmers' markets and is a favorite of chefs across the state. A tour of the ranch on a flatbed truck with Trish Strawn, winner of the University of Florida's Institute of Food and Agricultural Sciences Innovative Farmer of the Year award, is an educational hayride bar none. The conversations focus on farming practices that enhance, rather than harm, natural resources, and she speaks passionately about the ranch's relationships with chefs.

But the Deep Creek story is not only about what they do. It's about what they can do for others to support Florida's rich agricultural legacy. Deep Creek spends tens of thousands of dollars every year as a backup buyer for youngsters in 4-H steer and lamb programs. "We spread the net," says Trish's father, David, "so that these fine young people will receive the best possible price, above market, for the animal they hand-raised."

DEEP CREEK LAMB BURGERS

Lamb is a favorite of David's, and this recipe is a fresh take on the classic backyard hamburger. Try fresh thyme or mint in place of the basil, if you prefer.

SERVES 8

2 pounds ground lamb
1 red bell pepper, finely diced
1 yellow bell pepper, finely diced
1 cup finely chopped sweet yellow onion
3 tablespoons chopped fresh basil
1 garlic clove, minced
½ teaspoon coarse salt
¼ teaspoon freshly ground pepper
8 whole-grain hamburger buns, split, buttered, and toasted
8 tomato slices, for serving
8 lettuce leaves, for serving

1 Combine ground lamb, bell peppers, onion, basil, garlic, salt, and pepper in a large bowl. Stir to combine, being careful not to overmix. Shape into 8 (½-inch-thick) patties.

2 Grill until internal temperature reaches desired doneness: 145°F for medium-rare, 160°F for medium, or 170°F for well done.

3 Place each burger on bun, top with tomato, lettuce, and top half of bun.

HEIRLOOM COUNTRY FARMS

ARCHER

"Oh, you want to go for a swim, is that it?" Katharine Lune picks up a black-footed goose that's squawking at her feet and carries her over to a large trough with a hose attached to it. With a heave, Katharine tosses the big bird into the water. "She loves to swim, but she always wants me to help her get in the pool," Katharine says with a laugh. Her familiarity and nurturing instinct are present with all of the animals she raises, from geese, chickens, and guinea fowl to pigs, cows, and goats.

When Katharine and her husband, Rob, bought this land, she says they wanted to do something that would help pay for the property but also be a way to contribute to their community. Farming seemed like the right choice, Katharine says, even though she didn't have any prior experience. (Katharine runs the day-to-day operations at the farm; her husband is a web developer.) "I figured it out as I went along," she says. "We kept adding to our farm until we found the right balance with all the animals."

Among the farm's residents are Gloucestershire Old Spot pigs, an endangered heirloom breed noted for a higher fat-to-meat ratio than conventionally raised pork. Many consider the meat to be more flavorful because of the marbling. Katharine says it's important to her to keep this heritage breed going. "We're really trying to preserve the history of long-forgotten but really wonderful pigs."

PORK AND VEGETABLE STEW

This stew is best in the spring, when the potatoes, carrots, and herbs are young, but it can be served all year long. If you don't have a slow cooker, you can bake the stew in a covered Dutch oven at 250°F for 6 to 8 hours.

SERVES 6

1 (2- to 2½-pound) bone-in pork shoulder or pork sirloin roast

¾ teaspoon coarse salt

½ teaspoon freshly ground black pepper

4 tablespoons olive oil, divided

5 to 6 small potatoes

3 carrots, cleaned and chopped into 2-inch pieces

3 cloves garlic, peeled and smashed

2 stalks celery, leaves reserved, bottoms cut into 2-inch pieces

1 medium onion, cut into half-moon slices

⅓ cup all-purpose flour, seasoned lightly with salt and pepper

2 cups water, divided

3 sprigs fresh thyme, leaves removed and crushed lightly

1 to 2 large tomatoes, roughly chopped, or 14-ounce can diced tomatoes

1 to 2 bay leaves

1 loaf crusty French bread, for serving

1 Trim roast well to remove excess fat. Season pork generously with salt and pepper; set aside.

2 Heat 2 tablespoons oil in a large, heavy skillet over medium heat. Add potatoes, carrots, garlic, celery and celery leaves, and onion. Cook for 10 minutes, stirring, until vegetables are softened and golden brown. Transfer mixture to a slow cooker.

3 Heat remaining 2 tablespoons oil in the same skillet over medium-high heat. Add pork roast and sear each side until browned, about 12 minutes total. Remove roast from pan and coat in seasoned flour. Place roast over vegetables in the slow cooker.

4 Add ½ cup water to the skillet, place over medium-high heat, and deglaze pan, scraping any brown bits from the bottom. Pour into slow cooker.

5 Add thyme, tomatoes, bay leaves, and remaining 1½ cups water to slow cooker. Cover with lid, cook on low 6 to 8 hours.

6 Before serving, discard bay leaves. Remove pork roast and pull meat into large pieces. Discard bone. Serve with vegetables, broth, and crusty French bread.

PASTURE PRIME FAMILY FARM

SUMMERFIELD

Torm Siverson didn't set out in life to be a farmer, although it is clearly a lifestyle he knew well growing up in Marion County. Involved in 4-H programs in his youth, Torm and his siblings raised every kind of animal you can imagine. "You know, it's funny how things can change," says Torm. "I came back to help my parents ease into retirement and out of the dairy business, and in the process realized this was exactly where I wanted to be. My wife and I had been looking for a way to fit our philosophical ideas and environmental conscience into our lifestyle. We didn't need to look much farther than my own backyard."

Torm began researching Wagyu cattle, and in 2007, the first herd was grazing on the family farm. Torm also raises Mangalitsa and Berkshire pigs, heritage-breed turkeys, Label Rouge chickens, and eggs.

The new farm is sustainable, with an eye toward the future. "I have to credit the local restaurant chefs for being our best ambassadors," says Torm. Pasture Prime meats are found on menus at high-end restaurants throughout Florida. From 4-H to the forefront of modern farming, farm families such as the Siversons are charting a sustainable course for Florida agriculture.

PULLED PORK BANH-MI

Banh-mi is a traditional Vietnamese submarine sandwich that includes meat and crunchy vegetables. Tender and moist, pork shoulder (also called pork butt) stands in here for the more traditional barbecued pork, and Chinese five-spice powder—a blend of star anise, cloves, cinnamon, Sichuan pepper, and ground fennel—gives the meat a complex flavor.

SERVES 6

PORK

2 tablespoons packed dark brown sugar
2 tablespoons Chinese five-spice powder
2 tablespoons coarse salt
1 tablespoon coarsely ground black pepper
5- to 7-pound boneless pork shoulder

BRAISING LIQUID

1 cup chicken broth
¼ cup fish sauce
¼ cup lime juice
4 cloves garlic, smashed
2 shallots, thinly sliced
1 tablespoon sriracha (Asian hot chili sauce),
  or to taste

FOR SERVING

Baguette sandwich rolls
Sliced fresh jalapeños
Fresh cilantro
Sliced cucumbers

PREPARE THE RUB AND MARINATE THE PORK

1 Combine brown sugar, five-spice powder, salt, and pepper in a small bowl.

2 If there is a very thick section of fat on the pork, slice away some of it, leaving a moderate layer.

3 Rub spice mixture into pork shoulder until well coated.

4 Place pork in a medium roasting pan, cover with aluminum foil, and refrigerate overnight.

BRAISE THE PORK

1 Combine chicken broth, fish sauce, lime juice, garlic, shallots, and sriracha in a large measuring cup. Set aside.

2 Remove pork from refrigerator and set aside at room temperature for 30 minutes.

3 Preheat oven to 250°F. Uncover pork and pour braising liquid into roasting pan. Re-cover with foil and roast until an instant-read thermometer reaches 180°F, about 6 to 8 hours, depending on thickness of shoulder. Remove pork from braising liquid. Pour liquid in a fat separator, or skim excess fat from surface of liquid and discard.

4 Shred pork with two forks. Pile meat inside a baguette. Top with jalapeño, cilantro, cucumbers, and a drizzle of braising liquid.

Jim Wood

PALMETTO CREEK FARMS

AVON PARK

With just one bite, Jim Wood was on a mission. "The University of Florida invited some regional hog farmers to a dinner and meeting about meat-quality pork," says the family-farm owner. "They fed us pork from a wholesale club and a similar portion from the university's Swine Research Unit. The difference in meat quality was night and day. That night I drove home thinking about what I had to do to change our farm over from show pigs to meat-quality pork."

Palmetto Creek started with several breeds and crossbreeds, but Jim decided to narrow the scope down to the Hereford breed for the meat quality. In the end, the success of the new mission of Palmetto Creek depended on a couple of taste tests. "We developed most of the farm with the help of friends and family," he says.

A wine salesman who saw an article about the farm in a magazine introduced Jim to several chefs in the area, and they began to share their new find with customers and fellow chefs. "We found our market through the chefs," says Wood. "It doesn't make farming any easier, but it sure makes you feel good about what you are doing."

DRY-RUBBED BABY BACK RIBS

Dry rubs are easy to experiment with—use combinations of your favorite dried spices. Letting the ribs rest in the refrigerator, loosely covered, before cooking helps the dry rub adhere and imparts more flavor.

SERVES 4 TO 8

¼ cup packed dark brown sugar
¼ cup paprika
¼ cup ancho chili powder (dark Mexican chili powder)
4 teaspoons coarse salt
4 teaspoons smoked paprika
4 teaspoons cumin
4 teaspoons cayenne
4 (2-pound) slabs loin back ribs, membrane removed (ask your butcher or meat department to do this for you)

1 Mix brown sugar, paprika, ancho chili powder, salt, smoked paprika, cumin, and cayenne in a small bowl, making sure to break up chunks of brown sugar.

2 Put ribs bone side up on sheet pan. Season each slab with rub on both sides. Refrigerate at least 1 hour, loosely covered.

3 Heat oven to 250°F. Cut 4 (12-by-12-inch) square sheets of heavy-duty aluminum foil. Put a slab of ribs, meat side up, on a sheet of foil. Fold ends to make loose packet around each slab; seal. Put packets on sheet pan; bake 2 to 2½ hours. Check ribs for doneness by gently pulling on bones. When they begin to pull away from meat, they are ready to serve.

CITRUS GROWERS COOPERATIVES

FL

Citrus has been a bread-and-butter crop for Florida's farmers for more than a hundred years, and it remains a nearly $9 billion-a-year industry, according to the University of Florida's Institute of Food and Agricultural Sciences. Since the early twentieth century, growers' cooperatives have provided a way for family-owned farms to pool their harvests. As the citrus industry grew, co-ops became a way for the small farms to participate in the same markets as the large commercial growers.

Chances are, when you pick up a carton of orange juice, it will be made from a blend of juices from different farms across the state. Out of the four nationally branded juice marketers in the state, Florida's Natural Growers is the only one headquartered in the state. The Florida's Natural cooperative is made up of more than 1,000 growers, many of them multigenerational, family-owned farms. The cooperative concept allows members to share their cumulative experiences and knowledge to keep the citrus industry's roots running deep.

Chuck Gomez

PURE PRODUCE

MICCO

"You could call us a working salad bowl," says Chuck Gomez, who runs Pure Produce in Micco with his wife, Mayta. For more than 30 years, they've produced greenhouse tomatoes, baby English cucumbers, and an assortment of fancy lettuces.

Being a small farmer in Florida is hard work in a hard environment, says Chuck. The sandy soil, weather extremes, and pests attracted the couple to greenhouse farming. "You can grow clean crops in a greenhouse, and that's what attracts our regular customers at local co-ops and farmers' markets," says Chuck.

"The people who shop specialty markets ask questions about how we grow and why," Chuck continues. "As a farmer, I love that. I know that they understand how important it is to have a safe food supply and why it may cost a little more to have flavorful, clean food in their kitchens."

And with a greenhouse, he can experiment with a variety of seeds. Chuck's tomatoes, for instance, are from seeds from Holland—"expensive but worth it, with intense and memorable flavors," he says.

Pure Produce peppers, mushrooms, herbs, and more are at farmers' markets in Fort Pierce, Cocoa Beach, Palm Beach Gardens, and Melbourne. The farm also is part of Homegrown Co-op in Orlando.

TOMATO SALAD TONNATO

Oil-packed tuna and ripe tomatoes are the centerpiece of this dinner in a bowl, a riff on the classic Niçoise salad.

SERVES 4

1 pound (2 large) ripe tomatoes
6-ounce can oil-packed tuna, undrained
⅔ cup extra virgin olive oil
¼ cup red wine vinegar
2 anchovy fillets
1 tablespoon capers
2 teaspoons dried oregano
2 teaspoons dried basil
½ teaspoon coarse salt
½ teaspoon smoked paprika
¼ teaspoon freshly ground black pepper
Bibb or red-tipped lettuce leaves
4 hard-boiled eggs, cut in half
2 cups sliced cooked potatoes

1 cup cooked green beans
8 large kalamata olives

1 Core tomatoes and cut into wedges; set aside.

2 Remove 1 cup of tuna and set aside.

3 Combine oil, vinegar, anchovies, capers, oregano, basil, salt, paprika, pepper, and remaining tuna and its oil in food processor. Process until smooth; set dressing aside.

4 Line serving platter with lettuce leaves. Arrange eggs, potatoes, green beans, olives, tomato wedges, and reserved tuna on lettuce.

5 Spoon dressing over salad and serve immediately.

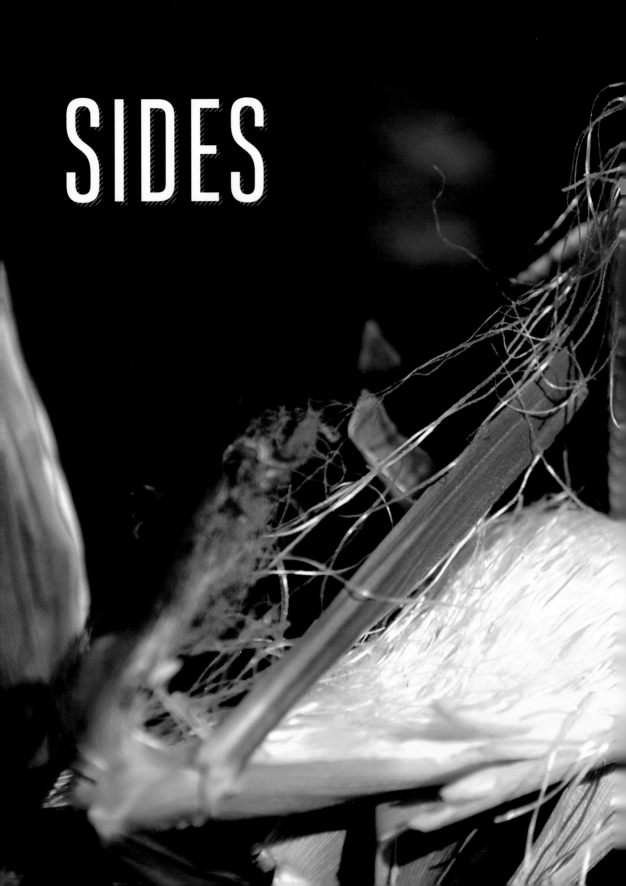

SIDES

RESTAURANT ORSAY

CHEF BRIAN SIEBENSCHUH AND
CHEF/OWNER JONATHAN INSETTA, JACKSONVILLE

"The idea of the chef who goes to the market every morning is, at least in Florida, a myth," Chef Brian Siebenschuh of Restaurant Orsay says. "Instead, we work with the farms in our area to source fresh, responsibly raised ingredients." Brian collaborated with noted Jacksonville restaurateur Jonathan Insetta to open Restaurant Orsay in 2006. The two have worked together since opening to ensure that the food served comes from high-quality ingredients, many of which are grown or raised within a few miles of the restaurant.

"I firmly believe in the relationship of the farmer with the chef," Jonathan says. "It allows for a greener footprint, finer-quality ingredients, and it allows us to create seasonally driven menus. It truly is a win-win."

In 2010, Jonathan invested in a joint venture in East Palatka to create Black Hog Farms. "The goal is to supply our restaurant and a few others with superior-quality products from a local farm," Jonathan says. He and Brian purchase as many ingredients as possible from the growing number of Jacksonville-area farmers. "My goal is to bring extremely high-quality and heirloom products to the consumer at an approachable price point," Jonathan says. "It is a rare opportunity to be part of a movement that has true substance, and we feel blessed to be part of it."

CHILLED HARICOTS VERTS WITH CRÈME FRAÎCHE VINAIGRETTE AND HAZELNUTS

When the spring season begins, haricots verts (thin green beans) and petite red onions are among the first tender produce available at Orsay. Tossing the beans in this creamy vinaigrette enhances their delicate flavor.

SERVES 4

1 pound haricots verts
¼ cup crème fraîche
2 teaspoons red-wine vinegar
¼ teaspoon coarse salt
¼ teaspoon ground black pepper
1 small red onion, thinly sliced
10 grape tomatoes, halved
¼ cup chopped, toasted hazelnuts, for garnish
Chopped fresh chives, for garnish

1 Fill a large bowl with ice and water; set aside.

2 Blanch haricots verts in salted, boiling water 1 to 2 minutes, or until just tender but still crisp. Transfer beans to ice bath and set aside.

3 Whisk together crème fraîche, vinegar, salt, and pepper in a large bowl. Set aside.

4 Dry beans with a kitchen towel and place in bowl with dressing. Add onion and tomatoes. Toss until well coated. Top with hazelnuts and chives before serving.

Facing: From left, Chef Brian Siebenschuh, front-of-house manager Crystal Vessels, and chef/owner Jonathan Insetta

FL

Bill and Pam Pischer run Desoto Lakes Organics and Jessica's Farm Stand, one of the oldest organic farms in Southwest Florida and a magnet for home cooks and chefs from Sarasota to Tampa. "We feel strongly that food is not a commodity," says Bill. "It's a living thing that should be treated with respect."

Bill's passion is that of a preacher called to convert a malnourished flock. He speaks of food in a spiritual sense with a measured sense of urgency. He is encouraged by what he describes as a "growing domestic trend that is embracing sustainable farms" from coast to coast. "A large segment of the population has forgotten their relationship with their food," says Bill.

Bill began his crusade in 1978. At first, he leased a few acres. Eventually, he bought the land. The stand he named after daughter Jessica. Today Bill and his wife, Pam, and all four of their children keep working to ensure food connections are restored, with a diverse showcase of seasonal produce including broccoli, carrots, cauliflower, celery, bell peppers, beans, and tomatoes. The whole family is dedicated to helping others find their path to rediscovery of the American food supply.

ZUCCHINI CARPACCIO

If you have a mandoline or V-slicer, this is the time to use it. If you don't, use a very sharp knife to slice the zucchini as thinly as possible.

SERVES 4

2 medium zucchini, stem tops and bottoms
   removed, sliced paper-thin
½ lemon, zested and juiced
2 tablespoons extra virgin olive oil
Coarse salt and freshly ground black pepper,
   to taste
4 basil leaves, torn into small pieces
4 mint leaves, torn into small pieces
¼ cup crumbled feta cheese

Arrange zucchini slices on a serving plate. Sprinkle with lemon zest and juice, then drizzle with oil. Season with salt and pepper and evenly distribute herbs over the plate. Top with feta.

SUPERGANIC FARM

PENSACOLA

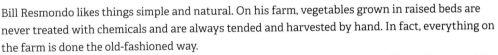

Bill Resmondo likes things simple and natural. On his farm, vegetables grown in raised beds are never treated with chemicals and are always tended and harvested by hand. In fact, everything on the farm is done the old-fashioned way.

Bill uses biodynamic methods, treating the soil as a living organism in itself. His "brown gold" compost contains nutrients that feed the soil, which in turn feeds the plants. "Healthy soil makes healthy plants, and healthy plants make healthy humans," he says. "It's that simple." With more than thirty-five years of experience in health and wellness, and as a spry septuagenarian, Bill would know.

The naturally grown, gargantuan heads of collard greens and bowling ball–sized yams are still more evidence of the fact that Bill is doing something right with his farming methods. "Superganic is a step beyond organic," he says. He claims that his commitment to biodynamics and his proprietary compost blend yield superior specimens—and when you see his larger-than-life Tuscan kale and lettuces, you might just agree.

CILANTRO-LIME KOHL SLAW

Bill's kohlrabies (also known as German turnips) can sometimes grow to the size of softballs. They have a mild, sweet flavor and crisp crunch, and they make an unexpected base for this refreshing slaw. You can substitute plain yogurt for the mayonnaise, if desired.

SERVES 4

½ cup mayonnaise
1 lime, juiced
½ teaspoon coarse salt
¼ teaspoon freshly ground black pepper
Dash hot sauce
½ large bunch fresh cilantro, roughly chopped
2 kohlrabi heads, peeled and shredded
2 carrots, peeled and shredded
1 green bell pepper, cut into thin matchsticks
1 jalapeño pepper, cut into thin rounds
  (optional)

1 Whisk together mayonnaise, lime juice, salt, pepper, and hot sauce in a small bowl. Stir in cilantro and set aside.

2 Combine shredded kohlrabi, carrots, green pepper, and jalapeño (if using) in a large bowl. Top with dressing and toss to combine. Refrigerate for at least 30 minutes before serving.

CHEF PAULA DaSILVA

MIAMI

With a farm-to-table restaurant on trendy South Beach in Miami, Paula DaSilva is part of the newest generation of chefs and a rising star in Florida's culinary circles. A native of Brazil, she started peeling garlic and cleaning vegetables in her family's restaurant as a teenager in Massachusetts. When the family moved to South Florida, Paula attended the Art Institute of Fort Lauderdale for a degree in culinary arts.

Today she's chef at 1500° in the historic Eden Roc Renaissance Hotel, for which she says freshness and seasonality are the keys to success. "I think cooking should be fun," says Paula. "I love using fresh ingredients and dedicating them to a dish from a region of the world where I feel like taking my guests."

Florida farmers are the soul of her kitchen, says Paula. "Without them, we wouldn't have the quality we need every day," she explains. "I have a very close relationship with all of my farmers and have visited just about every farm that I work with in South Florida."

Paula also nurtures her own garden at the restaurant, with everything from eggplant and radishes to spinach and beans. "The garden is always evolving," says Paula. "Florida has an amazing growing season, especially winter and spring."

SPICY SMOKED BABY POTATO SALAD WITH GARDEN GREENS, BRAISED BACON, AND SUNNY-SIDE-UP FARM EGGS

SERVES 6

POTATO SALAD

2 pounds baby rainbow potatoes
1 bay leaf
1 tablespoon black peppercorns

5 sprigs fresh thyme
½ head garlic
Coarse salt, to taste
1 cup wood chips
1 cup mayonnaise

1 small yellow onion, diced small and sautéed

3 calabrese peppers in oil, seeds removed and
sliced very thin

1 bunch scallions, sliced thin

1 tablespoon red-wine vinegar

Freshly ground black pepper, to taste

BACON

1 pound slab hickory-smoked bacon, unsliced

1 onion, chopped

1 large carrot, chopped

2 stalks celery, chopped

½ head garlic

10 sprigs fresh thyme

1 bay leaf

Coarse salt

1 teaspoon whole black peppercorns

2 quarts chicken stock

GREENS

1 pound fresh hearty greens, such as mustards
or chard

2 tablespoons olive oil

3 cloves garlic, minced

FOR SERVING

6 farm eggs

Olive oil, as needed

MAKE THE POTATO SALAD

1 Place potatoes in a large pot with bay leaf, peppercorns, thyme, garlic, and enough cold water to cover by 2 inches. Season well with salt and bring to a boil for 2 minutes, until just knife tender.

2 Remove from heat and cool potatoes in liquid. Drain and cut in half.

3 Meanwhile, build smoker: Soak wood chips in water for 30 minutes. Line bottom of a large pot that can be fitted with a perforated container (such as a steamer basket) with foil. Drain wood

chips and place them on the foil in bottom of pot, cover, and place over medium heat. When chips begin to smoke, place potatoes in perforated container into pot and seal with a lid or foil.

4 Smoke potatoes for 10 to 20 minutes, until desired smokiness is achieved.

5 Cool potatoes completely and mix with mayonnaise, sautéed onions, calabrese peppers, scallions, and red-wine vinegar. Season to taste with salt and pepper.

BRAISE THE BACON

1 Preheat oven to 300°F. Place all ingredients in a baking dish and cover with foil.

2 Braise in oven until tender when a knife is inserted, about 3 hours.

3 Remove from oven and cool in liquid for 1 hour, then remove and cool completely.

4 Slice bacon into thick strips. When ready to serve, reheat on a hot grill or under broiler.

COOK THE GREENS

1 Roughly chop greens and wash very thoroughly to remove dirt.

2 Heat a large sauté pan over high heat. Add olive oil and garlic and cook for 1 minute until garlic is just starting to color. Add the greens and cook, turning often, until wilted, about 5 minutes.

TO SERVE

1 Heat a large non-stick sauté pan over medium-high heat. Add a small amount of oil to coat.

2 Crack eggs into pan, keeping them separate. Season with salt and pepper. Cook until white is just set and remove from pan.

3 Repeat until all eggs are fried, and serve with hot sautéed greens, grilled bacon, and smoked potato salad.

CHEF MICHAEL SCHWARTZ

MICHAEL'S GENUINE FOOD & DRINK, MIAMI

"We have a 'spice route' going in Florida," says Chef Michael Schwartz. "We'll piggyback beef from Deep Creek Ranch, eggs from Lake Meadow Naturals, and they make their way to Wild Ocean Seafoods, who brings the goods south—everyone helping each other."

Michael has been cooking since he was fifteen and describes his food as an East Coast version of California cuisine. He sources exceptional ingredients from local producers and allows the ingredients and season to dictate the dish. He opened Michael's Genuine Food & Drink in Miami's Design District in 2007 with an unpretentious menu that showcases the bounty of Florida. The restaurant quickly rose to the top of many a food critic's list. In 2010, Michael was named Best Chef in the South by the James Beard Foundation.

The restaurant has a full-time employee whose job is to search for undiscovered farmers and artisans in Florida. "We have a commitment to supporting local agriculture," Michael says. "To really walk the walk isn't cheap or easy, or convenient, but I know if we don't support the small farmers, they'll disappear."

The unusual fruit in this recipe, the hua moa plantain, is cultivated by a handful of small growers in South Dade County. Some Cuban fruit stands in Miami occasionally carry hua moas, which they call plátanos hawainos.

HUA MOA TOSTONES

Michael says: "I've had some good tostones, but never anything like this. What happens when the rare hua moa plantain hits hot oil is a thing of greatness. Crispy on the outside and creamy sweet on the inside. After testing a few different methods in the kitchen, here's what we found to make the best. There are few ingredients, but very specific steps to follow in order for these to come out just right."

MAKES 12 TO 16 TOSTONES

Unripe (green) hua moa plantains, peeled and
    sliced into 1½-inch rounds
Vegetable oil, for frying
Coarse salt, to taste

1 To peel plantains, make one shallow slit lengthwise, just through skin. Place split plantains in boiling water for about 1 minute, or until skin turns brown. Remove and place in ice bath; peel and discard skin. Slice peeled plantain into 1½-inch rounds.

2 Heat 4 inches of oil to 350°F in an electric fryer or deep pot. If you don't have a deep-fry thermometer, a good way to test if oil is hot enough is to stick the end of a wooden spoon or chopstick in it. If bubbles circle around the end, oil is ready.

3 Fry plantain rounds all together about 1½ minutes, or just until they start to turn golden. Remove from fryer with a slotted spoon and transfer to an aluminum bowl. Cover with plastic wrap and let rounds sit 5 minutes. Leave oil at temperature on stovetop.

4 Place one round at a time, cut side up, on center of a lightly oiled wooden cutting board. Using both hands on each side, take another small oiled board or flat surface and press down evenly, flattening plantain round to ½-inch thick disc. Carefully lift top board. The plantain disc will now be about 3 to 4 inches in diameter. To remove, carefully slide a chef's knife under disc and transfer to a plate. Repeat, placing sheets of parchment paper between layers of plantains.

5 Fry discs, this time in batches of 3 or 4, without crowding, 2 to 3 minutes, or until golden brown. With tongs, transfer plantains to paper towels to drain. Season generously with salt and serve immediately.

SWALLOWTAIL CSA

ALACHUA

Noah Shitama and Zach McLean usually can be found with soil under their nails and sweat on their brows—and that's exactly why they cofounded Swallowtail CSA. In the largely agricultural town of Alachua, just up the road from Gainesville, Noah and Zach cultivate a beautiful farm with rows of colorful vegetables like ruffled red-violet lettuce, flowering broccoli, and deep purple–green kale. "We love to be outdoors, working in the dirt," Noah says. "I've always enjoyed working with my hands, but I came out here because I really wanted to connect with the land."

The land the farm occupies is a stretch of twenty acres that belong to Rick and Jane Nesbit, who allow Noah and Zach use of the land rent-free. They currently cultivate six acres. "The land itself is like a gift to us," Noah remarks. "We consider it a blessing to be here, and we owe that to [the Nesbits'] generosity."

The produce grown at Swallowtail is distributed solely through a CSA, which Noah says helps facilitate the feeling of community that was another driving force behind founding the farm. "We set out to create a cooperative of local farms and people," Noah says. "We really just want to reintroduce people to where food comes from."

SPICY-SWEET KALE

The combination of sweet balsamic vinegar and fiery horseradish complements the slightly spicy flavor of fresh curly kale.

SERVES 4

¼ cup chopped pecans
1½ pounds fresh curly kale
2 tablespoons unsalted butter, divided
4 tablespoons balsamic vinegar
3 green onions, minced
3 to 4 tablespoons prepared horseradish

1 Place pecans in a large sauté pan over medium heat. Toast until lightly brown and fragrant, shaking the pan frequently, about 3 to 4 minutes. Set aside.

2 Remove any tough center stems from kale, if necessary. Chop kale leaves into pieces slightly larger than bite-sized.

3 Heat 1 tablespoon butter in a large sauté pan over medium-high heat. Add kale and cook, stirring occasionally, until tender, about 5 minutes. Turn off heat and set pan aside.

4 Combine remaining 1 tablespoon butter, vinegar, green onions, and horseradish in a small bowl. Add to pan of kale, off the heat, and toss until kale is coated. Sprinkle with chopped pecans before serving.

SATUR FARMS

Palm Beach County's Satur Farms is the southern outpost of the original, on the North Fork of Long Island, New York, where in 1997 superstar chef Eberhard Müller and his wife, Paulette Satur, bought a small piece of land to grow produce for his Manhattan restaurant, Lutèce. When other high-end restaurants started clamoring for their produce, the two gradually began full-time farming in Cutchogue, New York.

Now it's a year-round endeavor with Satur Farms in Palm Beach County, where they head when the northern weather turns cool in September, farm until spring, and make Satur a "solid specialist," says Paulette. "We always have a crop, and we work year-round, seven days a week. It's how I grew up."

How did two high-powered New Yorkers get back to the basics of farming? Paulette grew up on her family farm in Central Pennsylvania, studied horticulture and plant physiology, and landed in the wine business in New York City. German-born Eberhard was a chef in top restaurants in Paris and Manhattan, including Bayard's, Lutèce, and Le Bernardin. They became weekend farmers when they married in 1996, but the garden quickly burgeoned into a full-time specialty farm. Paulette left her job first, then Eberhard departed as chef at Bayard's in 2005 and joined her in the business—a multistarred chef providing other chefs with beautiful kitchen bounty.

Today they farm more than 180 acres in New York and 144 acres in Florida, supplying top-tier restaurants and small grocery stores. On the Florida farm, the harvest includes delicate baby mesclun, wild arugula, spinach, butterhead and lollo lettuces, frisée, baby bok choy, radishes, baby Tokyo turnips, Swiss chard, baby beets, baby carrots, colored cauliflower, and herbs.

BABY TURNIPS AND CIPOLLINI ONIONS

"Eberhard's creations are always based on what is fresh and available from the fields," says Paulette. This recipe features tender baby turnips from their Florida farm along with small, sweet cipollini onions, which add depth to the dish.

SERVES 4

3 (8-ounce) bags cipollini onions, peeled and
   trimmed
1 tablespoon unsalted butter
1 teaspoon sugar
Coarse salt and freshly ground black pepper,
   to taste

3 to 3½ pounds (about 8 or 9 bunches) baby
   turnips, peeled and trimmed
½ cup water
Fresh herbs, for garnish

1 Peel onions by immersing in boiling water for a few minutes. Remove with a slotted spoon to a colander, cool slightly, then slip off and discard skins. Set onions aside.

2 Melt butter in a large saucepan over medium-low heat. Add sugar; season with salt and pepper. Cook until butter starts to turn golden brown, about 1 minute. Add turnips and onions, swirling pan to evenly coat. Add water, cover, and cook until almost all water has evaporated and vegetables are glazed, about 20 minutes.

3 Remove cover; continue cooking until liquid has evaporated and vegetables are caramelized, 3 to 5 minutes. Season with salt and pepper. Transfer to a large serving platter and garnish with fresh herbs.

FULL EARTH FARM

QUINCY

A brick red, open-sided barn and beautiful vegetable garden belie the fact that the land the farm sits on was once mined for the clay used to make cat litter. "Seriously," farmer Katie Harris says with a laugh. "The clay is called fuller's earth; our farm name is a tongue-in-cheek version of that."

Today grass covers the once-bare bowl-like dips in the ground. Honeybees bop in and out of brightly colored beehives (Katie painted the hive boxes a cheery poppy pink hue), making trips back and forth from the rows of vegetables, including "a lot of southern staples," she says. The neat rows are planted according to botanical family or the plants' needs, to allow for efficiency in water and compost use.

All of this is fairly new to Katie, who studied art and didn't have any prior experience in farming. A few years ago, she says, she had a "crazy plan" to come back home to Tallahassee and farm the land where her parents live in the neighboring town of Quincy. First, she took a year to work with Turkey Hill Farm, learning everything she could about farming, particularly natural growing practices. When she approached her parents with the idea of starting the farm, "it turned out that they had been wanting to farm the land, too," she says, "so it worked out well."

Katie and her partner, Aaron, along with a number of volunteers, keep the farm going year-round, harvesting garlic, onions, carrots, radishes, squash, green beans, peas, cabbage, corn, and much more.

ROASTED BROCCOLI WITH LEMON AND PARMESAN

One of the best-looking and heartiest crops Katie and Aaron grow is broccoli, with dusty green crowns surrounded by deep green leaves. Roasting the broccoli gives it a nutty flavor that's perfectly paired with shaved Parmesan cheese. A spritz of lemon juice brightens the whole dish. Don't discard the stalks on farm-fresh broccoli—if the broccoli is fresh, the stalk is tender and tasty. Peeling away the top layer eliminates any stringiness.

SERVES 4

1 large or 2 small heads broccoli
2 tablespoons extra virgin olive oil
½ teaspoon coarse salt

½ teaspoon coarsely ground black pepper
1 lemon, zested and juiced
½ cup shaved Parmesan cheese

1 Preheat oven to 425°F. Line a baking sheet with parchment paper; set aside.

2 Separate broccoli crown and stalk. Cut crown into bite-size florets. Peel stalk with a vegetable peeler and cut into ½-inch-thick strips.

3 Toss florets and stalk strips with oil in a large bowl. Add salt and toss to coat. Pour broccoli onto prepared baking sheet.

4 Roast 20 minutes, tossing once or twice, until broccoli is tender and dark brown in places.

5 Transfer roasted broccoli to a large bowl. Add pepper, lemon zest, and 1 teaspoon lemon juice. Toss to combine. Transfer broccoli to a serving bowl and top with shaved Parmesan.

REDLAND MEDITERRANEAN ORGANICS

REDLAND

Hani Khouri skillfully maneuvers a herd of playful Nubian goats across the front yard of his Redland home, shepherd's hook in hand, Goliath the rooster flapping his wings, and a goofy potbelly pig named Clementine snoozing in a corner.

It's a long way from Hani's pressure-cooker life as a Microsoft executive in Saudi Arabia. In 2005, he, wife, Mary Lee, and their children escaped the international fast track and moved to South Florida, where Mary Lee grew up. "And I feel like a kid again," says Hani.

Hani grew up in Lebanon, where he observed goatherders and learned the tradition of artisan cheese making from his mother. His own herd at Redland Mediterranean Organics seems to love South Florida's heat and produces milk rich in butterfat during the milking season between March and September.

He makes several types of goat cheese such as kishta, a soft, creamy cheese; kashkaval, a soft, fresh cheese; feta; haloumi; spicy shankleesh; a ricottalike arish; and several hard aged cheeses. Some are made in a day, others take months.

Exotic varieties of ice cream include avocado, green tea, papaya, and wild orchid, made with only three ingredients: goat's milk, fresh organic fruit, and agave nectar.

PURPLE CABBAGE AND GOAT CHEESE SAUTÉ

This sauté of purple cabbage, toasted walnuts, balsamic vinegar, and creamy goat cheese creates a warm salad that's loaded with antioxidants and vitamin C. The dish's red-violet hue is irresistible.

SERVES 4

½ cup walnuts
2 tablespoons extra virgin olive oil
½ head purple cabbage, thinly sliced
Coarse salt and freshly ground black pepper, to taste
2 tablespoons balsamic vinegar
1 tablespoon packed dark brown sugar
½ cup crumbled soft goat cheese

1 Toast walnuts in a nonstick skillet about 5 minutes, stirring often, until slightly browned and fragrant. Set aside.

2 Heat oil in a large nonstick sauté pan over medium-high heat. Add cabbage and season with salt and pepper. Stir in vinegar and brown sugar; sauté about 5 minutes, or until just crisp-tender.

3 Remove from heat and toss with goat cheese and walnuts. Serve warm.

ALGER FARMS

HOMESTEAD

Mason and Dorothy Alger arrived in Homestead from Massachusetts in 1934 and purchased 200 acres to plant snap beans, potatoes, and sweet corn. Their son, Richard, still an infant when they headed south, went on to become a Yale-educated plant scientist and one of South Florida's most successful agriculturists. His son, John, a Cornell University graduate, now runs Alger Farms, with the fourth generation, John W., a recent University of Florida master's degree graduate, working with his dad.

The Algers approach farming as a business and are great supporters of agricultural research and industrywide interests. And those 200 acres have grown to 1,100 acres of sweet corn, making Alger Farms a major provider of sweet corn in America's "winter bread basket."

SOUTHERN FRIED CORN

John says his favorite way to eat corn is "right out here in the field." His wife, Carla, says this recipe is John's favorite down-home dish. Once you toss the corn in the skillet, it begins to caramelize—be careful not to overcook, or the corn will toughen.

SERVES 4

6 ears fresh corn
4 slices bacon, halved
½ cup whole or 2% milk
1 teaspoon salt
¼ teaspoon pepper
Pinch of sugar

1 Cut corn kernels from cob with a sharp knife. Scrape the back of the knife blade down each cob to get all the milky pulp; set aside.

2 Fry bacon in a heavy skillet over medium heat until crisp. Remove bacon from skillet, reserving drippings, and drain on paper towel. Crumble bacon and set aside.

3 Add 4 tablespoons reserved bacon grease to same skillet. Add corn, cooking over medium heat without stirring until crisp on one side. Stir in milk, salt, pepper, sugar, and reserved bacon; cover and cook on low for 10 more minutes. Serve hot.

OLD-TIME FLORIDA CRACKER FAVORITE

Swamp cabbage is a vegetable cut from the heart of the cabbage palm. The plant, also known as palmetto palm, sabal palm, and swamp cabbage tree, is protected from indiscriminate cutting by its designation as Florida's state tree.

Cabbage palms clustered on private property and palms on land destined for clearing are fair game. Without these cuttings, fresh swamp cabbage would be hard to come by. The canned hearts of palm sold in grocery stores can be substituted in many recipes, but the products are imported from Central and South America.

The art of cooking swamp cabbage can be traced back to early Florida crackers, so named for the cracking of their whips on cattle drives. Living off the land was simply a way of life, and, with some work, swamp cabbage yielded a ready-to-eat delicacy reminiscent of asparagus or artichokes.

To harvest the tender heart, the tree is cut down, and about 3½ feet of the base is saved for the creamy-colored core. Getting to the core requires stripping away the exterior woody bark. Once the bark is stripped, the heart might weigh as little as 10 pounds.

Not all hearts of palm are equally tasty. The quality varies according to the age of the tree, its growing conditions, and the length of time between harvesting and processing. Perfect swamp cabbage is crunchy and tender without being fibrous.

Recipes for cooked swamp cabbage call for simmering chunks of the core with salt pork or other seasonings until the swamp cabbage is soft. Other cooks like to add the chopped hearts to fritter batters, or blend it with egg and other vegetables and fry in small patties. For purists, simply sliced raw and tossed into salads is the only way to enjoy swamp cabbage.

*Bill Dreggors of DeLand trims
fresh swamp cabbage*

FLORIDA SWAMP CABBAGE

You can't substitute canned hearts of palm here, but you can look for fresh swamp cabbage in specialty markets and at fish camps.

SERVES 8 TO 12

4 tablespoons unsalted butter
2 cups diced sweet onions
Coarse salt, freshly ground black pepper, to taste
1 tablespoon chopped garlic
3 cups water
3 pounds fresh swamp cabbage (hearts of palm)
1 cup white wine
¼ cup finely chopped fresh basil
2 tablespoons chopped chives

1 Melt butter in a large saucepan over medium heat. Add onions and season with salt and pepper. Cook, stirring often, until onions are translucent, about 5 minutes. Add garlic and sauté for 1 minute. Add water and bring to a boil. Add swamp cabbage.

2 Reduce heat to medium-low; simmer until swamp cabbage is tender, about 1 hour. Remove from heat and stir in the wine, basil, and chives. Season to taste with salt and pepper, if needed.

MARJORIE KINNAN RAWLINGS

SHE LOVED A GOOD DINNER PARTY

FL

Marjorie Kinnan Rawlings was one of Florida's great writers of native culture. Her words painted vivid images of life here in the 1930s, eloquent passages that hold up to this day.

In 1928, with a small inheritance from her mother, Marjorie and her husband, Charles, purchased an orange grove near Hawthorne, in a community called Cross Creek. The Pulitzer Prize–winning author chronicled her new life and that of others in rural Florida in such books as *South Moon Under, The Yearling,* and *Cross Creek.*

Her passion for food is clear in her writings. We get to know her characters through their struggles for sustenance and grace in the unforgiving hammocks and riverways. Marjorie introduces us to Fatty Blake's squirrel pilau in *Cracker Chidlings.* We meet moonshiners in *South Moon Under.* And in *Cross Creek* she notes, "The Ritz and the Waldorf and such haunts also serve our most exotic vegetable. They call it hearts of palm, but to us at the Creek it is, simply, swamp cabbage."

In addition to immersing herself in the culture and customs of those who lived near her homes in Cross Creek and Crescent Beach, Rawlings was a renowned hostess and cook. Many historians feel she never gave enough credit to her faithful workers, who taught her much about the land and how to make the most of harvests. Marge, as she was known to her close friends, loved a good dinner party. She compiled her favorite recipes for entertaining and more in *Cross Creek Cookery.*

"We need above all, I think, a certain remoteness from urban confusion," Marjorie writes in *Cross Creek.* Those words today could easily describe the family farms—small and large—that are hiding in plain sight throughout the state.

Today Marjorie's home at Cross Creek is a state historic site, where visitors can still walk through and see her small kitchen, her vegetable garden, and nearby citrus groves, preserved to capture the essence of Rawlings's simple life in North Central Florida.

SMOKY GOUDA GRITS

These grits were served at a dinner during the filming of Equinox Documentaries' *In Marjorie's Wake,* which has aired nationally on many PBS stations. Chives can stand in for the green onions, if desired.

SERVES 4

3 cups water
1 to 2 teaspoons coarse salt
14.75-ounce can cream-style sweet corn
¾ cup quick-cooking grits
1 cup fresh sweet-corn kernels
½ cup finely chopped green onions
1 garlic clove, minced
Shredded smoked Gouda, to taste
3 ounces cream cheese, softened

1 Bring water, salt, and cream-style corn to a boil in 3-quart saucepan. Gradually whisk in grits. Return mixture to a boil, whisking constantly.

2 Reduce heat to low; cover and simmer 5 to 7 minutes, stirring occasionally, until thickened.

3 Remove from heat. Stir in corn kernels, green onions, garlic, and cheeses. Serve hot.

Pulitzer Prize-winning author Marjorie Kinnan Rawlings chronicled Florida rural life from her home in Cross Creek

DUDA FARM FRESH FOODS

OVIEDO

Perry Yance

The Duda family has been tilling Central Florida soil since 1926, when Andrew Duda, a Slovak immigrant, and his three sons sowed the seeds for what is now a diversified land company that stretches from Florida to Texas, California, and Michigan.

Although the scope of Duda's business interests is now global, Oviedo has been home base for their operations for more than eighty-five years. And the company still is family owned, with the fourth generation at the helm.

Celery was the first Duda commercial crop, and it remains a primary commodity—the company has the world's largest celery research breeding program. Among its creations is the Dandy celery straw, a stalk with a hollow center that the company is promoting as an edible Bloody Mary swizzle stick, and red celery, a variety marketed under the brand name Celery Sensations, with a distinctive red wine–tinged base and the same flavor as regular celery.

Today the Duda corporate umbrella covers several divisions, including citrus and vegetables, sugarcane, and cattle. "We are proud of our long history in Central Florida agriculture," says David Duda, chief executive officer, "and we plan to continue growing our business for future generations to come."

COUSCOUS WITH CELERY AND PISTACHIOS

Citrus and fresh parsley add bright flavor, while celery and pistachios add pops of celadon green and welcome crunch to this easy side dish, perfect for a busy weeknight.

SERVES 6

10-ounce box couscous

2 teaspoons ground cumin

2 teaspoons minced fresh ginger

1 teaspoon ground coriander

½ teaspoon coarse salt, plus additional to taste

¼ teaspoon freshly ground black pepper, plus additional to taste

Pinch cinnamon

2 cups boiling water

2 oranges, zested, peeled, seeded, and cut into segments

1 cup chopped pistachios

¾ cup diced celery

2 tablespoons chopped parsley

2 tablespoons extra virgin olive oil

1 lemon, zested and juiced

1 tablespoon chopped green onion

1 Combine couscous, cumin, ginger, coriander, salt, pepper, and cinnamon in a medium bowl. Add boiling water. Cover bowl with plastic wrap and let stand 30 minutes.

2 Fluff couscous with a fork. Fold in orange zest, orange segments, pistachios, celery, parsley, oil, lemon zest, lemon juice, and green onion, mixing well. Add salt and pepper to taste. Set aside at room temperature for 30 minutes before serving.

TASTE OF OLD ST. AUGUSTINE

ST. AUGUSTINE

Small, yellow, and fiery hot, datil peppers are deeply rooted in both St. Augustine culture and the culture of the local Minorcans, descendants of immigrants from the Spanish island of Minorca, who have been living in St. Augustine since the 1700s. It's believed that the peppers most likely came from the Caribbean, but they grow only in Florida today. Datils, which are in the same family as super-spicy habaneros but with a sweeter flavor, are heavily used in Minorcan cooking. Though the peppers are not widely grown commercially, many St. Augustine residents have a plant or two in their backyards.

The late Jerry Millen, a botanist, used datil peppers as a way to cultivate interest in St. Augustine and Minorcan history and traditions. He grew the peppers on his farm and created a business of selling datil-based sauces and spices.

In 2004, Craig and Barbie Raynor took the reins, carrying on Jerry's company as Taste of Old St. Augustine, a division of their specialty-foods business. "Our mission is to foster awareness of our great, ancient city through the creation of wonderful-tasting products," Barbie says. The products include two types of hot sauce, barbecue sauce, two marinades, a spice blend, and other seasonal products, which are made in small batches using locally raised ingredients.

MINORCAN BLACK BEANS

Piquant datil peppers give a spicy kick to the Raynors' recipe for black beans—a staple in Minorcan cooking.

SERVES 6

1 pound dried black beans
1 ham hock
¼ cup olive oil
3 red or green bell peppers, diced
3 cloves garlic, minced
2 onions, diced
¼ pound Spanish chorizo sausage, sliced
¼ cup sherry vinegar or red-wine vinegar
4 bay leaves
½ fresh datil pepper, minced, or 1 teaspoon datil
   hot sauce
Coarse salt and freshly ground black pepper,
   to taste
Cooked white rice, for serving
Chopped raw onion, for garnish
Chopped fresh parsley, for garnish
Datil hot sauce, for garnish

1 Soak beans in cold water to cover overnight. In the morning, drain beans and place in a large stockpot with ham hock and enough water to cover by 2 inches. Do not add salt.

2 Simmer, partially covered, over low heat 3 to 4 hours, until beans are tender, adding water as necessary to keep beans submerged.

3 Meanwhile, heat oil in a large sauté pan over medium heat. Add bell peppers, garlic, and onions and sauté until softened, 4 to 5 minutes.

4 When beans are tender, add cooked vegetables, chorizo, vinegar, bay leaves, and fresh datil or datil hot sauce. Add salt and pepper to taste.

5 Simmer, covered, 1 hour to blend flavors. Add water, if necessary, so beans do not become too thick or dry.

6 Serve beans over cooked white rice and garnish with onion, parsley, and extra datil hot sauce on the side.

MONTEREY MUSHROOMS

ZELLWOOD

With operations around the world, Monterey Mushrooms is a second-generation family-owned agricultural business that started in 1971 in Royal Oaks, California. Today there are ten farms throughout North America, with a Florida outpost in Zellwood.

Every day, Central Florida employees nurture a dark, spongy blend of rolled wheat straw, protein meal, gypsum, and moisture to produce one of nature's most delicate edibles: the mushroom. You could call it compost deluxe.

The mushrooms are produced by full-tilt container gardening. The growing medium is carefully cultivated and aerated outdoors (with machinery reminiscent of a Mad Max fleet) before being added to large wooden boxes. The spongy mass is pasteurized before being seeded with spawn, tiny inoculated grains that eventually metamorphose into the prized mushrooms that creative cooks covet. At its peak growing stage, a mushroom begins to double in size every twenty-four hours. In Zellwood, inventory turns over every twenty-four to forty-eight hours.

While Monterey has international marketing cachet, it is serious about its locally grown mission, with a weekend mushroom market in the parking lot so locals can purchase the ultrafresh fungus.

MUSHROOM MEDLEY POTATO CAKES

To prepare fresh mushrooms for cooking, wipe them dry with a damp cloth or soft brush to remove dirt and trim stems if dry or tough. These quick cakes can be served as a side at breakfast or brunch, and they are a great use for leftover mashed potatoes.

SERVES 6 TO 8

1 thick slice bacon, diced
1 garlic clove, minced
1 shallot, finely chopped
2 cups chopped mixed mushrooms (such as white button, crimini, or portobellos)
2 cups peeled, cooked Yukon Gold or red creamer potatoes, grated or riced, and cooled
1 egg, beaten
1 teaspoon Dijon mustard
1 tablespoon chopped fresh chives
Coarse salt and freshly ground black pepper, to taste
1 cup panko (Japanese breadcrumbs)
Vegetable oil, for frying
Pesto, avocado slices, or fig chutney, for serving

1 Cook bacon 1 minute in a sauté pan over medium-high heat. Add garlic and shallot and cook 1 minute. Add mushrooms and cook, stirring often, 5 minutes, or until all liquid in pan is evaporated.

2 Remove pan from heat and stir in potatoes, egg, Dijon, and chives. Season to taste with salt and pepper.

3 Place panko in a shallow pie plate and heat oil for frying in a large skillet. Shape mushroom mixture into 6 to 8 balls and flatten each with a flour-dusted spatula. Coat flattened balls in panko, shaking off excess. Refrigerate for about 20 minutes to firm.

4 Remove from refrigerator and fry each cake 3 to 4 minutes each side, or until golden brown and heated through. Drain on paper towels and serve hot with pesto, avocado slices, or fig chutney.

SLOW FOOD USA ARK OF TASTE: DELICIOUS FOODS IN DANGER OF EXTINCTION

Slow Food is a global grassroots movement with thousands of members that links the pleasure of food with a commitment to community and the environment. To qualify for the Ark of Taste, a food must be at risk biologically or as a cultural tradition; be linked culturally or historically to a specific region, ethnicity, or traditional production practice; have outstanding taste, defined in the context of local traditions and uses; and have sustainable market potential.

According to the Slow Food USA website, the following Florida foods are on the Ark of Taste:

• **Florida Cracker cattle**. Florida Cracker is one of the oldest cattle breeds in the United States. The breed is descended from Spanish cattle that were brought to the New World beginning in the early 1500s and is known as a criollo breed because of its European origin. Florida has been a leader in the conservation and promotion of this breed over the past few decades. However, the breed is still quite rare, and increased knowledge about it is vital for its preservation.

• **Hatcher mango**. The Hatcher mango is a cultivar unique to South Florida. The Hatcher was developed by John Hatcher in Palm Beach County in the 1940s, and though there are probably hundreds of backyard trees in addition to his grove in Lantana, the Hatcher has remained relatively unknown among the large commercial mango growers in South Dade County. The Hatcher grove is at high risk because the four-acre property is threatened by encroaching development and obstacles like high property taxes and hurricanes, which have wreaked havoc among many longtime fruit grove owners in South Florida.

• **Tupelo honey**. Tupelo honey is produced when honeybees collect nectar from the blossoms of the white Ogeechee tupelo (Nyssa ogeche) tree. These trees are distributed along the borders of rivers, swamps, and ponds that are frequently inundated, mainly in the remote wetlands of South Georgia and North Florida. Tupelo honey is said to come from trees along just a few rivers, the most prominent (and generally agreed upon) being the Apalachicola and Ochlockonee. The strictly regional nature of tupelo honey dictates that its production exists in a tiny subculture.

• **Datil pepper**. Most visitors to St. Augustine have never heard of St. Augustine's most beloved treasure, the datil pepper, but it has been the centerpiece of Old Florida cuisine since the 1800s. The greatest challenge facing the small-scale datil pepper producers is the low quantity of peppers grown, since almost all production is centered around St. Augustine. The hurricanes and floods of recent years have been a considerable detriment to crops, and only a handful of farmers can meet commercial demand. Locals, however, continue to grow the pepper in their gardens and use it to make various hot sauces and other dishes.

• **Wilson Popenoe avocado**. The Popenoe avocado was imported from Tela, Honduras, in 1929 by Wilson Popenoe and from the Lancetilla Botanical Garden and Research Center in Honduras by H. F. Winters in 1966 to Miami. No one has done more to popularize the avocado in the United States than Wilson Popenoe. Avocado diversity is now threatened not only by global market demands for Hass avocados but also by the rapid spread of non-native, invasive pathogens for which

Wild Gulf Coast shrimp

the avocado has no natural resistance. Only three Popenoe avocado trees are thought to exist in Miami and Honduras today. There is one report of a grove in Venezuela that produces Popenoe avocados. The Popenoe avocado symbolizes the unique agricultural history of Miami and the extraordinary diversity of the avocado.

• **Wild Gulf Coast shrimp**. Wild Gulf Coast shrimp are wild-caught or free-range from the Gulf Coast of the United States, where they naturally exist. These shrimp are all warm-water species recognized for their sweet taste, firm texture, and crunchy meat. Aside from their color, the different varieties of the wild Gulf Coast shrimp are very similar. The white shrimp have grayish-white shells that turn pink when cooked; the brown shrimp have light brown or tan shells that turn coral when cooked; and the pink shrimp have light pink shells with a pearl-like texture that turn a deeper shade of pink when cooked.

• **Pantin mamey sapote**. A unique tropical tree fruit with an interior texture that is both creamy and sweet, the vibrant salmon-colored flesh of the Pantin mamey sapote is unlike anything most people have ever tasted. The flavor is a combination of sweet potato and pumpkin with undertones of almond, chocolate, honey, and vanilla. This superior mamey sapote cultivar was discovered growing near a fire station in Key West. The seeds of this tree are believed to have come from Cuba by way of nineteenth-century dissidents who left the island at that time. The small local farms where the Pantin variety is grown are now under siege from uncontrolled land development, hurricane damage, ever-rising property taxes, and escalating land prices.

• **Royal Palm turkey**. The Royal Palm turkey is listed as "Threatened" in the American Livestock Breeds Conservancy's Conservation Priority List. This list defines a threatened variety as having fewer than 1,000 breeding birds in the United States with 7 or fewer primary breeding flocks. These varieties are considered globally endangered.

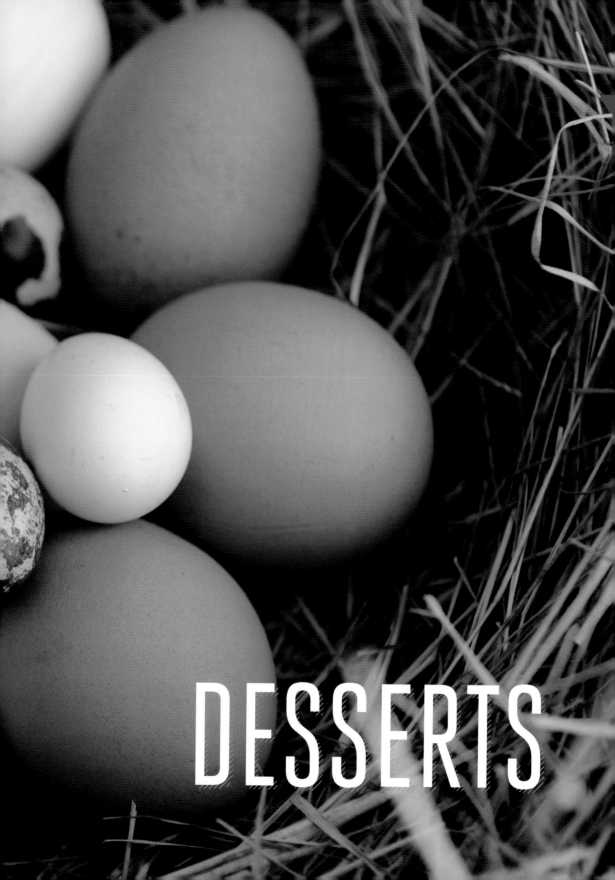

DESSERTS

WYNN HERITAGE FARMS

MADISON

Melvin Wynn didn't always want to work on the family farm. Though the six generations before him worked as farmers, Mel had a different plan—he left home after graduation and studied to become a jeweler. For thirty years, he cut and polished gemstones, designed one-of-a-kind jewelry, and traveled around the United States. "The older I got, though, the more I realized I wanted to get back to my roots," he says.

His roots were in Madison, a small town just outside of Tallahassee. He moved back to the home where he was born and reared, and started farming. Throughout the years, his family's farm had produced crops from tobacco and grains to cattle and hogs, but Mel decided to stick to fruit and vegetables. And though he has sporadic help, he does the lion's share of the work by himself, tending to rows of corn, pole beans, tomatoes, watermelons, and lettuce, among others.

The vegetables are available through a CSA, but many of Mel's customers are businesspeople in town who clamor for fresh produce when he swings by their offices. "My customers are like family," Mel says. "They each have a stake in what I'm doing here."

WATERMELON-ROSE ICE POPS

Mel's watermelon is one of the most sought after crops he offers in the summertime. These frozen pops combine sweet, ripe watermelon with a touch of floral rose water for a refreshing hot-weather treat.

MAKES ABOUT 12

6 cups large-diced watermelon, seeds removed
¼ cup sugar
2 teaspoons rose water
2 teaspoons fresh lime juice

1 Place watermelon in a blender and puree until smooth. Strain puree through a fine-mesh sieve lined with cheesecloth, pushing on solids. Discard solids.

2 Combine watermelon juice and sugar in a medium saucepan over medium heat. Cook just until sugar is dissolved. Remove from heat and cool completely. Combine sweetened watermelon juice, rose water, and lime juice in a medium bowl and refrigerate until cold.

3 Pour chilled mixture into ice-pop molds. Freeze until solid, about 8 hours.

Florida
Grapefruit
$1.00/each

OCHEESEE CREAMERY

GRAND RIDGE

FL

"Dairying is a way of life," Mary Lou Wesselhoeft says with a proud smile. And she would know, having grown up on the same property she lives and works on today. Though the milking operation has grown ("we used to milk in a 10×10-foot barn"), the principles are still the same. "Cows are like my young 'uns," she says. "I'm very hands-on with the whole process. I know each girl, their temperament, the way they like certain things to be."

Mary Lou and her husband, Paul, bought the farm from Mary Lou's parents in 1989. Their herd of 100-plus Jersey cows grazes on fields of green grass, clovers, and wildflowers, which give the milk its signature rich, clean taste.

Until about 2008, the Wesselhoefts were selling their milk to a cooperative, but it eventually became financially impossible to keep running their operation the way they wanted to. So the Wesselhoefts decided to start processing and bottling the milk themselves. "We needed to be able to set our own fair price for the milk," Mary Lou says. "The only way to do that is to bottle and sell it yourself." The milk is pasteurized and bottled in glass, which Mary Lou says keeps the milk colder and therefore fresher. "Plus, we feel that milk just tastes better when it's in glass," she says.

Whole and skim milk as well as decadently delicious chocolate milk are offered from the storefront. Eventually, the Wesselhoefts also want to sell ice cream.

CHOCOLATE-CHIP ICE CREAM

The rich flavor of the Jersey cream needs very little in the way of flavoring—a smattering of dark chocolate chips is just right. The vodka helps keep the ice cream soft in the freezer. You can omit it, but if you do, try to eat the ice cream within a day of making it. (That shouldn't be hard to do.)

MAKES 1 QUART

6 egg yolks
½ cup sugar
Pinch of salt
2 cups heavy cream
1 cup whole milk
1 vanilla bean, split lengthwise
1 tablespoon plus 1 teaspoon vodka
6 ounces semisweet or dark chocolate, finely
 chopped

1 Whisk together egg yolks, sugar, and salt in a large bowl; set aside. Combine cream and milk in a small saucepan. Use the back of a small knife to scrape seeds from inside the vanilla bean. Add seeds and bean to milk mixture and place pan over medium heat; heat until tiny bubbles just begin to form around edges. Remove from heat for 5 minutes.

2 Fill a large bowl with ice and a bit of water; set aside.

3 Slowly ladle 1 cup of hot cream mixture into egg yolks, whisking constantly. Pour egg-cream mixture back into the saucepan and cook, stirring occasionally, until mixture coats the back of a wooden spoon, about 4 minutes.

4 Discard vanilla bean. Pour custard through a fine-mesh sieve into a medium bowl and set the bowl in the ice bath, adding water if needed to reach halfway up sides of bowl. Stir until custard is cool. Add vodka. Remove from ice bath and refrigerate for 2 hours, or until cold.

5 Freeze in an ice-cream maker according to manufacturer's instructions. When ice cream has the consistency of soft-serve, transfer to a freezer-safe container and stir in chopped chocolate. Freeze until firm.

*Chefs Julie and James Petrakis
with farmer Charley Andrews*

HAMMOCK HOLLOW

ISLAND GROVE

It's not easy to find the farm, but once you make the turn off the main road, a classic Florida farmhouse and rows of greenery let you know you're in the right place. Charley Andrews left the fast-paced technology scene in Silicon Valley to come back home to Florida and start a farm.

His all-natural techniques are well respected and emulated by other farmers, and Charley often hosts interns and apprentices who want to learn from his success. On seven acres, he grows a stunning array of vegetables, from plump San Marzano tomatoes to sweet-hot peppers to beautiful, fragrant melons.

Charley sells mostly to commercial buyers, and many of Central Florida's top restaurants rely on his beautiful vegetables, many of them heirloom varieties, for their menus.

CANTALOUPE SHERBET

There's nothing like farm-fresh, ripe cantaloupe. When the melon is almost overripe, it's perfect for this easy, super-refreshing sherbet. Limoncello, an Italian lemon liqueur, keeps the sherbet scoopable. You can omit it, though the sherbet will harden after a day or so in the freezer.

MAKES 1 QUART

1 large, very ripe cantaloupe, chopped
  (about 3½ to 4 cups)
½ cup sugar
1 tablespoon limoncello or citrus-infused vodka
½ cup heavy cream

1 Puree cantaloupe in a blender until smooth. Pour half of cantaloupe puree in a medium saucepan over medium heat. Add sugar. Cook, stirring, just until sugar is dissolved.

2 Remove pan from heat, pour puree into a large bowl, and cool to room temperature. Add second half of cantaloupe puree, limoncello, and heavy cream to bowl and stir to combine. Refrigerate until mixture is cold.

3 Freeze in an ice-cream maker according to manufacturer's instructions. Transfer to a freezer-safe container and freeze until firm.

CHEF BRANDON MCGLAMERY

LUMA ON PARK, WINTER PARK

Chef Brandon McGlamery of Luma on Park in Winter Park began his culinary training in the early '90s. He left Florida and ended up in Northern California, where the emphasis on regional cooking was strong thanks to the farm-to-table passion of one of Brandon's mentors, Chef Jeremiah Tower.

"Chefs often spent their weekends finding great suppliers and then trying to convince the farms to distribute to their restaurant," Brandon says. "That experience created the most important foundation that I still strive to achieve daily—seasonally directed and ingredient-driven menus." When he returned to Florida to take the helm at Luma, Brandon says he had a hard time finding suppliers right away who could fill the needs of a busy restaurant. "Over time that changed," he says. "I look forward to what the next generation of Florida farmers will produce for everyone in this amazing state."

"It's all about the ingredients," he adds. "It's the core of everything we do. Knowing my food sources elevates my passion as a chef. That core connection goes from the purveyor to the chef and to the customer."

FRESH BLACKBERRY MILKSHAKES

This icy indulgence is great for spring brunches or hot summer days. The combination of fruit and cream is a natural, and the addition of lime juice freshens the flavor with a subtle note of citrus.

SERVES 4 TO 6

1 pound fresh blackberries
¼ cup sugar
1 lime, juiced
1 quart premium store-bought vanilla ice cream
1 cup half-and-half

1 Combine blackberries, sugar, and lime juice in a medium bowl and set aside 30 minutes. Transfer mixture to a medium saucepan over medium heat and cook until berries soften and break down, about 5 minutes. Refrigerate until cold.

2 Combine ice cream, half-and-half, and chilled blackberry mixture in a blender. Blend until smooth.

Facing: Brandon McGlamery
with farmer Dale Volkert of
Lake Meadow Naturals

PAISLEY PECANS

PAISLEY

Ivan Jeffrey didn't plan to become a pecan farmer. Thirty years ago, his father, George, a farmer and veterinarian, retired from Bronson, Michigan, to Paisley, a small town on the edge of the Ocala National Forest. He bought 100 acres of land with a plan to plant citrus trees, but experts encouraged him to grow pecans, a crop that was not very well represented in the state at the time. The Jeffreys planted 400 pecan trees and irrigated the property, all by hand, and thus began a flourishing business.

Eventually, the work became too much, and George told Ivan that he planned to sell the farm. "He had tears in his eyes when he told me that he couldn't take care of the land anymore," Ivan recalls, "so I decided to help out." Every three weeks, Ivan would fly from his home in Michigan to Florida, where he'd mow the orchard and take care of chores. When his father passed away, Ivan bought the farm, and he and his wife, Nina, moved to Florida.

Though the trees aren't as prolific as they once were, Ivan says owning the farm has been enjoyable. "It's given me such an insight into my parents," he says. "My father's longtime customers have all these great stories to tell about him and my mom, which is pretty cool."

Those customers can still buy pecans at the farm, as they have for the past twenty-five-plus years. The trees don't have large yields, so the Jeffreys simply put a sign out on County Road 42, and people drive to the orchard to pick them up.

PECAN PRALINES WITH DARK CHOCOLATE AND SEL GRIS

People buying pecans at the farm love to share their favorite recipes, Ivan says, and pralines are one of the most popular. This one has bittersweet chocolate and just a hint of salt to counter their super-sweetness. Sel gris is a coarse French sea salt with a gray hue that comes from its mineral content. If you can't find sel gris, you can substitute any coarse sea salt.

MAKES ABOUT 20 PRALINES

2 cups whole pecans, divided
2 cups packed light brown sugar
½ cup heavy cream

2 tablespoons unsalted butter
6 ounces bittersweet chocolate, finely chopped
1 teaspoon sel gris

1 Line 2 baking sheets with parchment paper; set aside.

2 Chop 1 cup of pecans into pieces. Combine with 1 cup whole pecans and set aside.

3 Combine brown sugar, cream, and butter in a medium saucepan over medium-high heat. Bring to a boil and cook, stirring constantly, about 3 minutes. Add all the pecans and cook, stirring constantly, 3 more minutes, or until mixture is thick.

4 Remove from heat and cool for 5 minutes. Vigorously stir mixture with a wooden spoon until pecans are coated and mixture turns opaque.

5 Drop mixture by tablespoons onto prepared baking sheets. Cool completely at room temperature.

6 Place half of chocolate in a medium microwave-safe bowl. Cook in 30-second increments until mostly melted. Stir until melted and smooth, then add remaining chocolate, stirring until melted and smooth.

7 Drizzle pralines with chocolate. Sprinkle each praline with a bit of salt. Set aside to allow chocolate to harden.

SMILEY APIARIES

WEWAHITCHKA

On the banks of the Apalachicola River, the white tupelo tree blooms just three or four weeks a year in the spring, its pompomlike blossoms full of nectar that draw massive swarms of honeybees. They buzz from the trees to hives which beekeeper Donald Smiley strategically places close to the swampy areas where the trees grow, to get the highest concentration of pure tupelo nectar. The resulting honey is prized for its delicate flavor and because it is the only honey that will not crystallize.

In the tiny window during which the white tupelos bloom, Donald says the timing is critical to ensure his honey is as pure as possible. He strips the hives of any existing honey as soon as the first white tupelo trees begin to flower and must harvest the honey just as the blooms fade, to eliminate the presence of any other nectar.

Before he was a beekeeper, Donald was a commercial oysterman in Apalachicola Bay. In 1988, an interest in honeybees led to the purchase of a few colonies and, later, an apprenticeship with a local beekeeper. By 1996, Donald's initial eight colonies had grown to a few hundred, and beekeeping was his full-time job.

After the yearly harvest, Donald sends his honey to the Florida Department of Agriculture to test for the distinctively shaped tupelo pollen. "We're almost always 95 percent," Smiley says, "and that's about as close to pure as you can possibly get in nature."

TUPELO HONEY BAKLAVA ROLLS

Instead of making one big sheet of baklava, rolling the phyllo dough around the filling takes most of the tedious labor out of this delicious Mediterranean dessert. You can find orange blossom water in Mediterranean food shops.

MAKES 12 (3-INCH) SLICES

TUPELO HONEY SYRUP

1½ cups tupelo honey
¼ cup water
1 tablespoon orange blossom water

BAKLAVA ROLLS

2 cups chopped unsalted pistachios
2 cups chopped walnuts
½ cup confectioners' sugar
1 teaspoon orange blossom water

Pinch coarse salt
1 cup melted butter
20 (14x9-inch) sheets frozen phyllo dough,
    thawed

PREPARE TUPELO HONEY SYRUP

Combine honey, water, and orange blossom water in a small saucepan. Bring to a boil, lower heat, and simmer for 5 to 8 minutes, or until thickened slightly. Set aside to cool.

MAKE BAKLAVA ROLLS

1 Preheat oven to 275°F. Grease a baking sheet with butter; set aside.

2 Combine pistachios, walnuts, confectioners' sugar, orange blossom water, and salt in a medium bowl.

3 Place 1 sheet of phyllo on a work surface with the short end facing you and brush with melted butter. Keep remaining sheets covered with a slightly damp kitchen towel. Repeat, creating a stack of 5 sheets.

4 Place 1 cup nut mixture in a line at bottom of phyllo stack, on the short end, leaving a 2-inch border at bottom edge and sides. Carefully roll into a long cylinder. Carefully transfer roll to prepared baking sheet. Repeat process with remaining phyllo sheets and nut mixture.

5 Bake 1½ to 2 hours, or until golden brown. Cool 5 to 7 minutes, then pour prepared honey syrup over top. Cool completely before cutting into 3-inch pieces with a serrated knife.

LAKE MEADOW NATURALS

OCOEE

Lake Meadow Naturals is the home of a variety of heritage, rare, and unusual breeds of chickens and ducks that lay eggs in various shades. Roaming on the west Orange County farm are a huge array of chickens—black Australorps, Rhode Island Reds, buff Orpingtons, Araucanas, Phoenixes, turkens, Wyandottes, and Jersey Giants.

Dale Volkert runs the farm and says his business has steadily increased as more chefs and supermarkets have discovered his farm-fresh eggs hatched from free-roaming, hormone-free, grain-fed chickens. "People are really paying attention to what they are eating," he says. "But I am really amazed by the reaction of visitors here. We open the farm one day a week to the public. And the looks on the faces of not only the children but the adults, too, are astounding. It's as if they are seeing where food comes from for the first time."

Running the busy farm is not easy work, but Dale says they are encouraged every day by the farm-to-table connection they're making. "I grew up on a dairy farm. We had chickens and all kinds of animals running around. I guess I took it for granted that other people didn't have the same experiences."

SIMPLE LEMON CURD

You can add more sugar if you prefer a sweeter taste, but the Volkerts like this versatile sauce to be tangy. Use any leftover lemon curd the next day on your morning toast.

SERVES 4 TO 6

5 cage-free egg yolks
½ cup sugar
4 Florida lemons, zested and juiced (you should have about ⅓ cup juice)
1 stick unsalted butter, cut in pieces and chilled
Freshly whipped cream, for serving
Seasonal fresh berries, for serving

1 Fill a medium saucepan with a few inches of water and place over medium-high heat.

2 Combine egg yolks and sugar in a heat-proof bowl that's slightly bigger than the saucepan. Place bowl atop saucepan, being careful not to let bowl touch simmering water. Whisk yolks 1 minute, then add lemon zest and juice. Whisk 6 to 8 minutes, or until mixture thickens.

3 Remove from heat and add butter one piece at a time, stirring until fully melted before adding the next piece. Cool.

4 Serve lemon curd topped with whipped cream and fresh berries.

TROPICAL BLOSSOM HONEY CO.

EDGEWATER

Amid the 250,000-plus products at the annual Summer Fancy Food Show in New York City, there is always lots of Central Florida buzz, thanks to hard work over the years by Doug McGinnis and his sister, Patricia.

The family enterprise, Tropical Blossom Honey Co. in Edgewater (just south of New Smyrna Beach), was founded in 1940 by their parents, David K. and Helen McGinnis. David kept bees in the orange groves, swamps, and forests of Central Florida. Helen packed the bees' honey in jars, and they sold their hand-packed treasures up and down Florida's coasts.

At the 2009 51st Fancy Food Show, son Doug accepted a fifty-year plaque commemorating Tropical Blossom's long participation in the trade show. The company specializes in the thick, sweet elixirs that are uniquely Florida: orange-blossom honey, tupelo honey, palmetto honey, unfiltered tropical wild honey, and citrus honeys enhanced with the natural essence of Key limes and tangerines. "One hundred fifty-three companies showed honey at the 2009 show," says Doug. "For years, we were the only honey company in the show." Today Tropical Blossom still sells honey throughout the United States and to more than twenty countries around the world.

HELEN MCGINNIS'S HONEY BANUTTY DESSERT

Doug McGinnis remembers this family snack from his mother's kitchen. Today he often uses half-and-half instead of evaporated milk. This is even better served over homemade (or good-quality store-bought) chocolate ice cream.

SERVES 8

1 cup crunchy peanut butter
½ cup evaporated milk or half-and-half
½ cup orange-blossom or palmetto honey
4 bananas, peeled and quartered

1 Combine peanut butter, evaporated milk or half-and-half, and honey in a small saucepan over low heat. Cook, stirring, until ingredients are blended and warm.

2 Place two banana quarters in a small bowl and spoon warm sauce over them.

MAGGIE'S HERB FARM

ST. AUGUSTINE

If the breeze is blowing just so, you can smell it before you see it. On a stretch of land along the St. Johns River is Maggie's Herb Farm, a twenty-eight-year-old, pesticide-free farm that grows culinary and medicinal herbs, along with a few heirloom vegetables. Maggie Oulette, a gardener and plant collector, started growing herbs in her backyard in 1983. What began as a hobby quickly turned into a thriving business, and she eventually had to move from her backyard to the space where the farm is today. Trained herbalist Dora Baker, a longtime customer, took over the farm when Maggie retired in the mid-'90s, and she says she's still doing things the way Maggie originally intended.

"It might sound odd, but the whole reason I found Maggie's farm was because I was looking for bugs, and they were the only nursery or farm in town who had any to spare since they were pesticide free," she says with a laugh. "Maggie never used chemical sprays back then, and I'm proud to say we're still completely pesticide free."

The farm's 200 varieties include many hard-to-find herbs that are sought after by people from all over the country. "I love herbs because they are food and they are medicine," Dora says. She offers classes throughout the year on everything from herbal remedies for cold and flu season to cooking with herbs and encourages customers to think beyond the more familiar uses of the fragrant plants.

ROSEMARY-PECAN SHORTBREAD COOKIES

Though rosemary is often considered a savory herb, it's delicious in Dora's nutty shortbread cookies, giving them a pleasing herbal flavor. Be sure to use tender leaves and mince them very finely.

MAKES 3 DOZEN

1 cup unsalted butter, softened
¾ cup confectioners' sugar
1½ teaspoons rose water

Pinch of salt
2 cups all-purpose flour
1 tablespoon finely minced fresh rosemary
¾ cup pecans, chopped

1 Preheat oven to 350°F.

2 Combine butter, confectioners' sugar, rose water, and salt in a large bowl and beat with an electric mixer until light and fluffy. Add flour and rosemary to butter mixture, stirring until just combined. Stir in pecans.

3 Roll dough into 1-inch balls and place 2 inches apart on ungreased cookie sheet. Bake 20 minutes, or until golden.

4 Cool 10 minutes on cookie sheet, then cool completely on a wire rack.

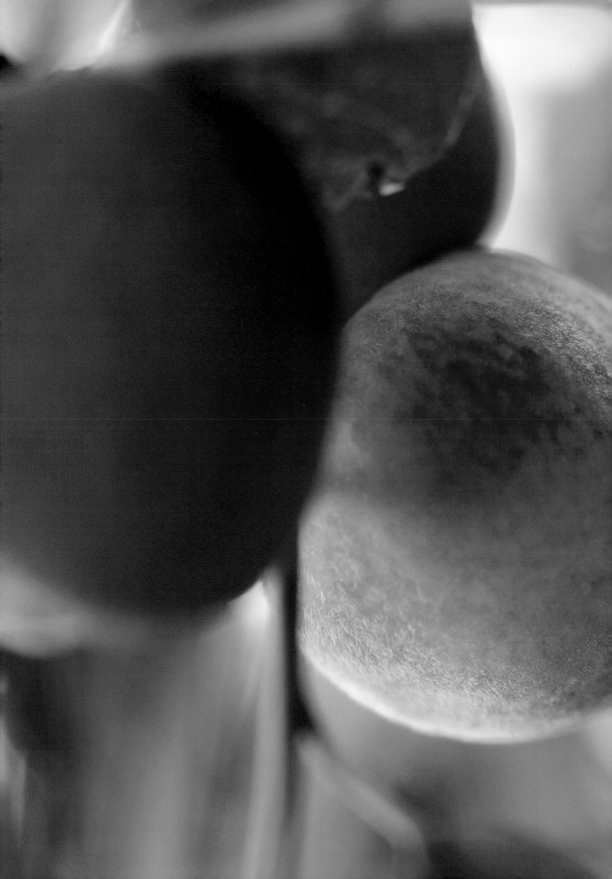

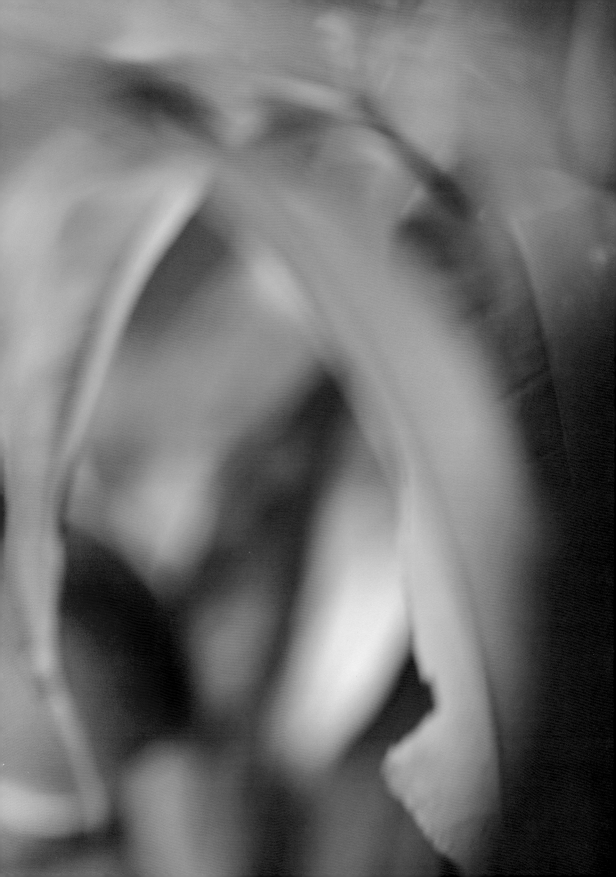

ORCHARD POND ORGANICS

TALLAHASSEE

At first glance, Orchard Pond Organics looks exactly how you might imagine a southern plantation would—dirt roads lined with moss-draped pine trees and handmade white fences leading to a flock of hens, a herd of cattle munching in the grassy field, and horses roaming freely in the green pastures.

Another look around reveals a colorfully painted Volkswagen van and a vintage Airstream trailer with a clothesline to its left—hallmarks of the offbeat, fun energy that Orchard Pond embodies. The Airstream is home to a full-time employee who tends the eight-acre vegetable plot, and the van transports the weekly market deliveries.

Farm owners Mary and Jeff Phipps decided in 2008 to start farming the 1,000 or so acres that have been in Jeff's family for generations. "We just felt that it would be the best use for all this land," Mary says. The farm received USDA Organic certification not long afterward.

The Phippses nourish more than 100 community members through their CSA, and many more through the family garden plots that border the farm's vegetable tract. For a small monthly fee, Tallahassee residents can have year-round access to a 50 × 30-foot plot that they can use to grow anything they like—as long as they adhere to the requests of the farm: no herbicides, pesticides, or genetically modified organisms. "We have loved getting to see people coming out to grow their own vegetables," Mary says. "It builds such a feeling of community."

PUMPKIN-GINGER SCONES

This recipe is inspired by one from Orchard Pond's farm manager, Mary Russ. Fresh pumpkin puree is easy to make—simply cut a small baking pumpkin in half, roast until soft, scoop out the flesh, and puree in a food processor. Strain excess liquid from puree if it seems thin.

MAKES ABOUT 14

1½ cups all-purpose flour

½ cup stone-ground whole-wheat flour

⅓ cup sugar

1 teaspoon salt

4 teaspoons baking powder

4 tablespoons cold unsalted butter, cut into small pieces

2 tablespoons vegetable shortening

⅓ cup fresh or canned pumpkin puree

½ cup heavy cream

1 egg

1 cup chopped crystallized ginger

1 Place a pizza stone or large rimless baking sheet on the middle rack of the oven and preheat oven to 375°F.

2 Combine all-purpose flour, whole-wheat flour, sugar, salt, and baking powder in a large bowl.

3 Add butter and shortening and rub with fingers until pea-sized bits form. Set aside.

4 Whisk together pumpkin puree, cream, and egg in a small bowl. Pour cream mixture into flour mixture and stir until just combined. Add ginger and knead with floured hands until dough just comes together.

5 Turn dough out onto a floured surface and roll out to ¼-inch thickness. Cut scones with a round cutter, rerolling scraps only once.

6 Bake, in batches if necessary so scones don't touch on baking sheet, until lightly golden, about 15 to 20 minutes.

Facing: A vintage Airstream trailer is farmer Jeremy Greer's home at Orchard Pond Organics

ERICKSON FARM

CANAL POINT

"All mangos are not created equal," says Dale Erickson, a fourth-generation mango farmer with forty acres of the sweet fruit on the southeastern shore of Lake Okeechobee. "Kent, Southern Blush, Bailey's Marvel, they all have their own personalities."

Erickson Farm, Inc., dates back to 1911, when Swedish immigrants Alfred and Elfrida Erickson and their four children started farming along the lake. Two of the sons, Floyd and William, continued farming vegetables until Floyd began planting mangos and avocados in the 1960s. In 1974, Floyd's son, Dale, took over the mango production and started growing other tropical fruit. Today Dale runs the farm with the help of his two daughters, Krista and Kim, and Krista's young son, Brendan, the fifth generation.

While they ship most of their mangos, a sixty-year-old mango tree in the front yard is their best advertising, with fans flocking to their roadside mango stand from June to October. The sixty-two-acre farm produces more than a dozen tropical fruits including avocados, carambolas, sapodillas, longans, lychees, and papayas, but mangos are their passion.

Shipping fruit may pay the bills, but Dale loves the customers who drive right to their front yard. "It's the way I was raised," he says. "I still remember selling mangos out of the back of my little red wagon."

MANGO COBBLER

Dale's favorite way to eat a mango is right off the tree, but a close second is his mother's recipe for mango cobbler.

SERVES 6 TO 8

4 cups mango, peeled, cut from the pit, and cubed
⅔ cup sugar
2 tablespoons cornstarch
1 tablespoon butter
Cinnamon (optional)

1 cup self-rising flour
1 tablespoon sugar
3 tablespoons shortening
½ cup whole milk
Whipped cream, for serving
Ice cream, for serving

1 Preheat oven to 400°F.

2 Cook mango and sugar in a medium saucepan over medium heat, stirring frequently, 8 to 10 minutes, until mango begins to soften.

3 Mix cornstarch in small amount of water in a small bowl and stir into hot fruit. Pour into ungreased 2-quart baking dish and dot with butter. Sprinkle with cinnamon, if desired.

4 Mix together flour, sugar, and shortening in a medium bowl with a pastry blender or two knives until mixture resembles coarse meal. Stir in milk and mix well. Drop by spoonfuls onto hot fruit.

5 Bake for 25 minutes, or until golden brown. Serve warm with whipped cream or ice cream.

GOING BANANAS

HOMESTEAD

Don and Katie Chafin were working in high-pressure jobs in Miami when they decided to leave the rat race behind and escape to historic Redland, "Dade County's last frontier," says Don. In 1986, the husband and wife bought a five-acre former lychee grove and started growing organic banana plants, aptly naming the venture "Going Bananas."

Today they sell more than ninety varieties of banana species, far beyond the familiar yellow Cavendish, such as the firm, fruity Nam Wa; the delectable Pisan Raja; the sweet, creamy Ice Cream; and the fragrant Rajapuri, with a hint of strawberry, "the most delicious banana you can sink your teeth into," says Katie.

Bananas grow as far north as Central Florida, and Don encourages home gardeners to start with a variety like Goldfinger, which ripens fast, has a lemony taste, and is resistant to disease.

BANANA BREAD PUDDING WITH ISLAND RUM SAUCE

Katie often cooks with the fruits of their labor, and this delectable bread pudding is a Chafin family favorite.

SERVES 6 TO 8

BREAD PUDDING

1 pound day-old French bread
4 cups whole milk
3 eggs
1 cup sugar
2 tablespoons vanilla
1 teaspoon ground cinnamon
Pinch ground nutmeg
4 ripe bananas, mashed

RUM SAUCE

2 tablespoons water
8 tablespoons butter
1½ cups sugar
¼ cup dark rum

MAKE THE BREAD PUDDING

1 Preheat oven to 350°F.

2 Tear bread into bite-sized pieces and place in a large bowl.

3 Whisk together milk, eggs, sugar, vanilla, cinnamon, and nutmeg in another large bowl.

4 Add mashed bananas to milk mixture and stir; pour over bread and let sit 20 minutes.

5 Pour into greased 9x13-inch baking dish and bake for 1 hour, or until golden.

MAKE THE SAUCE

1 Heat water in a small saucepan. Add butter and sugar and stir over low heat until sugar dissolves. Whisk in rum.

2 Just before serving bread pudding, drizzle sauce over top.

BURR'S BERRY FARM

MIAMI

A postcard-perfect roadside stand, white wood trimmed in red, baskets of beautiful produce, homemade jams, and pots of blooming flowers—Burr's Berry Farm has been a Redland tradition since 1965. Step up to the window for produce and you'll likely see Mary Burr, in her eighties, still smiling and greeting loyal patrons. A separate line forms for fresh-fruit milkshakes, an old-fashioned indulgence that draws a crowd on hot afternoons.

The Burrs were pioneers in Florida, arriving from the North in 1876. Charlie Burr was the next generation, born in 1922 in a home that remains unchanged today. Known in Redland as the "Strawberry King," he planted his first crop of berries in 1960. He loved ice cream and added strawberry ice cream and milkshakes to the roadside stand in 1968. The rest is history.

Daughter Kathy Burr Magee remembers "growing up here in a fairyland, where dad enjoyed flying his small plane around the Redlands." Charlie passed away in 2001, but the family, including his wife, Mary, still opens the stand each strawberry season from December to May, with thirty acres of berries just out the back door.

"It's been a way of life for us," says Kathy, "a good one."

MEMA'S GUAVA ROLL

"Guavas grew everywhere back then," Kathy says. This recipe is one of her favorites from her grand-mother, Carrie Hutchins Burr. "I remember her making guava jelly from the trees on the farm that were loaded with fruit in the summer."

SERVES 6 TO 8

GUAVA JELLY
2 pounds ripe guavas
1 cup sugar
3 teaspoons fresh lime juice

SPONGE CAKE
Unsalted butter, for greasing pan
1 cup flour, sifted 4 times
¼ teaspoon salt
½ teaspoon lemon zest
5 eggs, separated
1½ tablespoons lemon juice
1 cup sugar
Confectioners' sugar, for dusting

PREPARE THE JELLY

1 Cut blossom end off guavas and thinly slice.

2 Cover fruit with water and cook in a large pot over medium heat for about 1 hour, or until guavas soften. Allow fruit to cool in the water.

3 Strain the fruit through cheesecloth over a large bowl. Let juice drip several hours. Discard the solids.

4 Stir together 1 cup juice (reserve any remaining for another use), sugar, and lime juice in a saucepan over medium heat. Bring to a boil and cook for 8 to 10 minutes. The jelly is ready when it begins to coat the back of a spoon. Remove pan from heat and allow to cool for 30 minutes.

MAKE THE CAKE

1 Preheat oven to 325°F. Line a 15x10-inch jellyroll pan with parchment paper; lightly butter the paper. Set aside.

2 Sift together flour and salt in a small bowl. Add lemon zest; set aside.

3 Beat egg yolks and lemon juice in a small bowl until thick and lemon-colored; set aside.

4 Beat egg whites until stiff but not dry in a large mixing bowl. Gradually fold in sugar. Fold egg yolk mixture into egg whites. Gradually fold in flour mixture.

5 Pour batter into prepared pan. Bake for 15 minutes, or until cake is golden. Remove from oven and loosen edges of cake with a knife; invert onto a lightly dampened towel dusted with confectioners' sugar. Gently peel parchment paper off cake.

6 Trim ¼-inch of hard crust off each long side of cake. Beginning with narrow side, roll cake and towel up together. Cool cake on a rack, seam side down, for 10 to 15 minutes.

7 Once cake has cooled, unroll and spread with guava jelly; reroll. Dust with confectioners' sugar.

Facing: The Burr family, from left, Mary Burr, Kathy Burr Magee, and Judy Burr

CHESTNUT HILL TREE FARM

ALACHUA

Created in 1981 by Bob Wallace and his wife, Deborah A. Gaw, Chestnut Hill's roots run deep in the nursery business. Bob is the grandson of Dr. Robert T. Dunstan, an acclaimed plant-breeding pioneer. The elder Dunstan's lifelong interest in plant propagation led to remarkable accomplishments in the development of grapes and other horticultural science endeavors, according to the University of Florida's Institute of Food and Agricultural Sciences.

Those achievements included the Dunstan hybrid chestnut, a cross between a surviving American chestnut discovered in Ohio in the 1950s and USDA selections of Chinese chestnuts. In 1962, seedling trees from the first crossbreeding began to bear fruit. After selecting the trees with the most hybrid characteristics, the elder Dunstan then crossed them back to the American and Chinese parent trees. The resulting second generation was moved to the property where Chestnut Hill Tree Farm stands today, in North Central Florida. Those trees have been thriving and bearing nuts for more than fifty years.

Today Dunstan chestnuts are widely planted in the United States, making the Chestnut Hill Tree Farm a national leader in the developing domestic chestnut industry. While the farm also specializes in pecan, peach, and persimmon trees, berries, and many lush flowering trees, Chestnut Hill prides itself most on its chestnut heritage.

CHOCOLATE CHESTNUT TORTE WITH GANACHE GLAZE

Debbie Gaw says this is her family's favorite dessert, making an appearance on every holiday table. To roast chestnuts, preheat oven to 375°F. With a sturdy knife, cut an X or a deep slit into the rounded side of the chestnuts (this prevents the nuts from exploding in the oven). Roast on a baking sheet 15 to 20 minutes, or until you can pierce them easily with a fork.

SERVES 8 TO 10

TORTE

2 cups roasted, peeled chestnuts (see recipe
  introduction above)
4 tablespoons rum, preferably dark
1 stick butter
2 cups semisweet chocolate chips
6 eggs, separated
Pinch of salt
½ cup sugar

GLAZE

1¾ cups semisweet chocolate chips
½ cup heavy cream
1 tablespoon dark rum
Shaved sweet chocolate and freshly whipped
  cream, for garnish

MAKE THE TORTE

1 Heat oven to 350°F. Grease an 8- or 9-inch springform pan. Line with a round of parchment paper and dust lightly with flour. Set aside.

2 Combine chestnuts, rum, and butter in the bowl of a food processor, pulsing until mixture forms a smooth paste.

3 Place chocolate chips in a microwave-safe bowl and microwave in 30-second intervals until mostly melted. Stir until melted and smooth. Add melted chocolate to chestnut mixture, stirring to combine. Fold in egg yolks. Transfer mixture to a large bowl.

4 Beat egg whites in a separate large bowl with a pinch of salt. Once egg whites start to thicken, slowly add sugar, continuing to beat until stiff. Gently fold beaten egg whites into chestnut mixture just until no large white streaks remain. Do not overmix.

5 Pour batter into prepared pan. Bake 45 to 55 minutes, or until a knife inserted in the center comes out with only a few crumbs attached. Do not overbake. Set aside to cool for 20 minutes.

6 Invert torte and remove from pan. Remove and discard the parchment paper. Place top side up on a large plate to cool completely.

GLAZE THE TORTE

1 Place chocolate chips in a medium heat-safe bowl. Heat cream in a small saucepan over medium heat until it just begins to simmer. Immediately add hot cream to chocolate, stirring until smooth. Stir in rum.

2 Pour glaze over cooled torte and smooth with the back of a large spoon or an offset spatula, allowing some of the glaze to drip over sides. Set aside until glaze is firm. Garnish with shaved chocolate and whipped cream.

GREEN GATE OLIVE GROVE

JACKSON COUNTY

You might not expect anyone to compare the Mediterranean with Florida's Panhandle, but Don Mueller knows that in regard to weather, the two can be quite similar. In 1999, he started an experimental farm growing one of the Mediterranean region's specialties: olives. Don, who lived and worked in Europe for many years, took frequent trips to Italy with his wife, where their favorite hotel was set in an olive grove. When the Muellers retired to Florida, Don says he set his sights on olives for something to keep him busy. "Everyone said it couldn't be done, but I did it anyway."

He began by importing numerous types of olive trees from overseas to see what would work. North Florida's sandy soil, mild winters, and warm summers turned out to be ideal for a handful of those varieties—one of which took seven years just to fruit. It took eight years before Don was ready for customers, but today the farm is home to some 300 trees and is the only farm in Florida with a significant yearly yield of olives.

The olives are available at the farm through U-pick, in ten-pound packages, or in jars of salty brine. Don also has a twenty-ton hydraulic jack that he uses to press batches of olives into fresh, peppery oil. It's delicious on its own as dipping oil with bread, but it's also outstanding in this simple cake.

OLIVE OIL CAKE

Don's olive oil lends a fruity flavor and moist texture to this cake. When blueberries aren't in season, serve the cake with a glaze made from fresh orange juice or lemon juice and powdered sugar.

MAKES 1 (8-INCH) CAKE

Baking spray with flour, for pan
1½ cups all-purpose flour
2 teaspoons baking powder
½ teaspoon salt
1 cup sugar
3 eggs

¼ cup whole milk
2 teaspoons orange zest
2 teaspoons orange liqueur
1 cup extra virgin olive oil
Powdered sugar, for sifting
1 pint fresh blueberries, for serving
Confectioners' sugar, for dusting

1 Preheat oven to 350°F. Spray an 8-inch round cake pan with baking spray with flour; set aside.

2 Whisk together flour, baking powder, and salt in a large bowl; set aside. Whisk together sugar, eggs, milk, orange zest, and orange liqueur until pale. Slowly whisk in olive oil.

3 Add sugar and egg mixture to flour mixture, stirring just until combined. Be careful not to overmix.

4 Pour batter into prepared pan. Bake 40 minutes, or until cake is golden and a wooden pick inserted in the center comes out clean. Cool in pan on wire rack 30 minutes, then invert onto a cake plate and cool to room temperature.

5 Dust with confectioners' sugar and serve with fresh blueberries.

LARSON DAIRY

OKEECHOBEE

Red Larson

When Red Larson was a youngster, he sold his pony to buy a cow, bottled the milk, and sold it to neighbors for ten cents a quart. Those auspicious sales launched a career that has lasted a lifetime for one of Florida's most respected dairy leaders.

Fast forward to Louis E. "Red" Larson, an air force pilot in World War II who came home to attend the University of Miami after the war. In the 1940s, he became partners with a friend who owned a dairy, married wife Reda, and settled into the business.

"We supplied Key West with all its milk in the late 1940s and early 1950s," Red says. "As the home of the navy base, [South Florida was] a strong customer."

Ebullient Red was always one to take a chance, and he moved northward and bought a dairy in Palm Beach County. As the state's population began to expand, he started buying other farms, and today the Larson Dairy empire, centered in Okeechobee, includes 15,000 acres and 10,000 cows. Milking is high tech with computerized machines and pipeline milking, and his two sons and a pair of grandsons are in charge of day-to-day responsibilities. "We're bigger today than we ever intended, but we expanded to stay competitive," Red says.

Red has been honored with many achievement awards, but one of his proudest moments was when his four children established three endowments at the University of Florida's Institute of Food and Agricultural Sciences in honor of their dad's leadership in Florida's dairy industry. The University of Florida also named a building in his honor, the L. E. "Red" Larson Dairy Science Building.

The octogenarian still rises at 5:30 a.m. and heads to the office for a full day. "If you enjoy what you're doing, why quit?" he says with a grin.

MRS. LARSON'S PEANUT BUTTER MERINGUE PIE

Reda loves cooking for their family and friends, and she says this old-fashioned peanut butter pie is always the most requested for church suppers.

MAKES A 9-INCH PIE

PEANUT BUTTER FILLING

1 cup sugar

¼ cup cornstarch

2 cups milk

3 egg yolks, lightly beaten

2 generous tablespoons smooth peanut butter

9-inch prebaked pie shell

MERINGUE

4 egg whites, room temperature

1 pinch cream of tartar

2 tablespoons sugar

PREPARE THE FILLING

1 Preheat oven to 350°F.

2 Stir together sugar and cornstarch in a heavy saucepan. Mix in milk and egg yolks. Cook over low heat, stirring constantly until sugar is dissolved. Bring to a boil and boil for 1 minute, or until mixture coats the back of a spoon. Remove from heat; stir in peanut butter.

3 Pour mixture into piecrust; set aside.

MAKE THE MERINGUE

1 Beat egg whites and cream of tartar with an electric mixer until foamy. Gradually add sugar, beating 1 to 2 minutes until meringue just holds stiff peaks.

2 Spread meringue over filling, making sure it touches all edges of crust. Draw meringue up into peaks and bake pie 10 to 12 minutes on middle rack of oven until meringue is golden. Remove from oven and cool completely on a wire rack before slicing.

SHADY ACRES STRAWBERRY FARM

DOVER

Eva Nell Griffin enjoys the regulars who flock to the small three-acre berry farm she and her husband, Russell, run in Hillsborough County. "I've had the pleasure of welcoming up to three generations of strawberry lovers during the harvest season," Eva Nell says affectionately. "I just love to watch the parents show their children the joy of fresh ripened fruit."

The native Floridian, one of nine children, grew up on a family farm and knows quite well the ins and outs of strawberries. "My father grew strawberries in the late 1940s and early 1950s. There have been a lot of changes since then. We picked all of the berries ourselves. The farm children went to school during the summer so we could help our families with the winter harvest. There was no hired help like today."

Eva Nell is quite content with the family U-pick operation. "We'll start checking the berries in late November and our season can run through to April," she says. "We have lots of wonderful trees on the property, so it's not unusual for groups to have picnics under the cool canopies. They pick a little, then rest a little and make a day of it. It's wonderful to watch."

Growing up in the thriving local berry industry, Eva Nell is, not surprisingly, partial to the flavor of local berries. "They just taste sweeter to me," she says without hesitation. "I don't think a strawberry from anywhere else in the world can beat a Florida strawberry."

OLD-FASHIONED STRAWBERRY PIE

This pie with its bright ruby color is a retro southern picnic favorite. Keep berries whole if they're small and arrange in circles in the crust.

SERVES 8 TO 10

CRUST

1 cup coarsely chopped pecans
¾ cup graham cracker crumbs
6 tablespoons melted butter
2 tablespoons sugar

PIE

1 cup water
⅓ cup sugar
2 tablespoons cornstarch
3-ounce package strawberry-flavored gelatin
4 cups sliced fresh strawberries
Freshly whipped cream and fresh mint, for garnish

MAKE THE CRUST

1 Heat oven to 350°F.

2 Combine pecans, graham cracker crumbs, butter, and sugar in a large bowl. Evenly press into a 9-inch pie pan. Bake 10 minutes, or until edges begin to brown. Remove from oven and cool completely.

MAKE THE PIE

1 Combine water, sugar, and cornstarch in a small saucepan, stirring until smooth. Bring to a boil; cook, stirring, for 2 minutes, or until thickened. Remove from heat; add gelatin, stirring until dissolved. Refrigerate 15 minutes.

2 Arrange strawberries in crust. Pour gelatin mixture over berries. Refrigerate until set. Garnish with freshly whipped cream and mint.

ROBERT IS HERE

HOMESTEAD

On a sunny Saturday afternoon, there's a traffic jam just off U.S. Highway 1 in otherwise quiet Florida City. A line winds out the door for tropical fruit milkshakes at Robert Is Here, a rowdy roadside market where shoppers fill baskets with tomatoes, corn, Key limes, papayas, mangos, tamarinds, carambolas, and other produce fresh from the field. Most days you'll find Robert Moehling smiling and chatting up regulars from behind the checkout counter.

Robert Is Here started in 1959, when six-year-old Robert tried selling his dad's cucumbers on the side of the road—and no one stopped. That evening, his dad decided that the passersby must not have seen his son, and the next day he placed a handwritten sign on each side of Robert's card table proclaiming in big red letters: "Robert Is Here." The signs worked. By noon, Robert had sold all the cucumbers and walked home. The following weekend another farmer added tomatoes to Robert's table, and the business was born.

For years, the school bus picked Robert up and dropped him off at the roadside stand. Mornings, he would set up an honor-system can for money, and each afternoon he would work his stand until dark. By age fourteen, he had bought his first ten-acre piece of property, planted an avocado grove there, and rented out the house on the property.

Fast forward to 2011, and Robert is still there, along with his two sons and two daughters, who have joined the business. Their small farm provides some of the produce for the market, but the open-air building now features an amazing array of tropical fruits and fresh produce along with shelves of chutneys, more than 100 jams and jellies, flavored honeys, bee pollen, relishes, hot sauces, homemade breads, pies, and more. Out the back door is Robert's menagerie of animals, from emus to donkeys and goats—an authentic roadside attraction on the edge of the Everglades.

CLASSIC KEY LIME PIE

"There's nothing romantic about Key lime pie," says Tracey Moehling, Robert's wife. "It's just an old-fashioned standard in our family." This version of the Florida favorite is inspired by Robert's recipe.

MAKES 8-INCH PIE

CRUST
1¼ cups graham cracker crumbs
2 tablespoons sugar
5 tablespoons unsalted butter, melted

FILLING
4 egg yolks
14-ounce can sweetened condensed milk
½ cup plus 2 tablespoons fresh Key lime juice

TOPPING
¾ cup chilled heavy cream

MAKE THE CRUST
1 Preheat oven to 350°F.

2 Stir together graham cracker crumbs, sugar, and butter in a bowl with a fork until combined. Press onto bottom and sides of 9-inch pie plate.

3 Bake on middle rack of oven 10 minutes; cool completely.

MAKE THE FILLING AND BAKE
1 Whisk together egg yolks and condensed milk. Add Key lime juice and whisk until mixture thickens slightly.

2 Pour filling into crust and bake on middle rack of oven 15 minutes. Cool completely, then refrigerate, covered, at least 8 hours.

MAKE THE TOPPING
Just before serving, whip cream with an electric mixer until stiff. Serve pie topped with cream.

*Facing: Robert Moehling, center,
and his sons at Robert Is Here*

CHEF MICHELLE BERNSTEIN

MICHY'S, SRA. MARTINEZ, MIAMI

"Kumquats, lychees, kale, and tomatoes," Michelle Bernstein says, ticking off her favorite Florida produce. An impressive array of fruits and vegetables take center stage on the South Florida superstar's menus, as Michelle believes that she has an obligation to support the state's farmers.

"It's my job to support those that help me do what I love to do," she continues. What's freshest on the farm influences her sublime Latin cuisine "with a little bit of the islands."

The professional ballerina–turned–chef is best known for the eponymous Michy's in Miami, along with The Crumb on Parchment and Sra. Martinez restaurants. In 2008, she was named Best Chef in the South by the James Beard Foundation, and she continues to make a splash on the national culinary scene.

"I cook the food I love," Michelle says, "and I think that love translates to diners."

MANGO UPSIDE-DOWN CAKE

Mangos are prolific in South Florida for nearly six months out of the year, and one of Chef Bernstein's favorite desserts enhances their sweetness by caramelizing the fruit.

MAKES 1 (9-INCH) CAKE

TOPPING

4 tablespoons unsalted butter

¼ cup packed light brown sugar

2 firm but ripe mangos, peeled, pitted, and sliced lengthwise into ⅜-inch-thick slices

3 tablespoons dark rum

CAKE

½ cup melted unsalted butter

¾ cup granulated sugar

¼ cup Florida honey

3 eggs

1½ cups all-purpose flour

2 teaspoons baking powder

1 teaspoon coarse salt

½ cup buttermilk

1 teaspoon vanilla extract

Fresh whipped cream, for serving

MAKE THE TOPPING

1 Melt butter in a small heavy saucepan over medium heat. Add brown sugar, then mango slices; stir about 3 minutes, or until golden brown and caramelized.

2 Remove pan from heat and, after a minute, stir in rum. Pour mixture into 9-inch round baking pan, overlapping mango slices.

MAKE THE CAKE

1 Preheat oven to 350°F.

2 Stir together butter, sugar, and honey in a large bowl, beating until combined. Add eggs and whisk until pale yellow and fluffy.

3 In a separate bowl, sift together flour, baking powder, and salt. In a third bowl, mix together the buttermilk and vanilla. With an electric mixer on low, alternately add flour mixture and buttermilk mixture into butter mixture until thoroughly combined.

4 Pour batter over mangos and bake for 35 to 45 minutes, or until tester inserted in center of cake comes out clean. Cool in pan on a rack for 10 minutes. Run a knife around edges to loosen cake and invert onto a platter. Serve with whipped cream at room temperature.

KNAUS BERRY FARM

HOMESTEAD

Brothers Ray and Russell Knaus started growing strawberries more than fifty years ago in Dade County's Redland, but it was the sweets created by Ray's wife, Barbara, that became legendary at Knaus Berry Farm. Knaus family members are Dunkers, a sect of German Baptists, and Barbara continued the Dunker tradition of baking authentic old-fashioned specialties made just as they were a century ago—delectable cakes, cookies, brownies, bread, and pies. But it's the gooey cinnamon buns that are the hallmark of the roadside stand.

Visitors make the trek to Knaus to pick their own plump strawberries and ripe tomatoes from mid-November to late April, but most every customer leaves with a fruit-flavored milkshake, slice of pie, cookie, or cinnamon bun right out of the oven. You may have to stand in line, but your patience will be rewarded.

CINNAMON BUNS

Barbara's son-in-law Tom Blocher has been running the little bakery for twenty-nine years and wouldn't part with the cinnamon bun recipe. So here's our version inspired by the Knaus favorite.

MAKES 1 DOZEN

DOUGH
3¼ cups flour
3 tablespoons sugar
½ teaspoon salt
¼ ounce active dry yeast
⅓ cup unsalted butter
⅔ cup milk
2 eggs

SYRUP
½ cup unsalted butter, room temperature
2 tablespoons turbinado sugar
4 tablespoons honey
3 tablespoons light corn syrup

FILLING
½ cup granulated sugar
1 cup turbinado sugar
2 tablespoons cinnamon
½ stick butter, melted

MAKE DOUGH
1 Lightly butter a 12-cup muffin pan; set aside. Line a baking sheet with parchment paper large enough to cover muffin pan; set aside.

2 Combine flour, sugar, salt, and yeast in a large mixing bowl.

3 Melt butter and milk in a saucepan over very low heat; remove from heat and whisk in eggs. Stir into dry ingredients, then knead for 5 minutes with dough hook on electric stand mixer. When dough is springy, form a ball and place in a greased bowl. Turn to coat and cover with plastic wrap. Leave in a warm place for 2 hours or until doubled in size.

MAKE SYRUP

1 Cream butter until soft with electric mixer; add sugar, honey, and light corn syrup.

2 Divide mixture into prepared muffin cups.

MAKE FILLING AND ROLLS

1 Preheat oven to 350°F. Mix together granulated sugar, turbinado sugar, and cinnamon.

2 Turn out risen dough onto a lightly floured work surface and punch down to deflate. Roll out to a rectangle (about 24-inches-by-12 inches) with the long side nearest you.

3 Coat dough with melted butter.

4 Sprinkle with sugar-cinnamon filling. Roll up starting with long side and pinching seam to seal, keeping a firm, elongated shape.

5 Cut with a sharp knife into 12 even slices and place in muffin cups. Let rise until almost doubled in size, about 30 minutes.

6 Bake 20 to 25 minutes until golden brown. Remove from oven, let cool for 5 minutes, then place parchment-lined baking sheet on top of muffin pan; turn cinnamon buns onto baking sheet.

BLUE BAYOU FARMS

YALAHA

Doug and Amanda McCormack started their Lake County family farm in 2007. Doug has been in the wholesale business for many years as a partner in his family's McCormack Nursery in nearby Howey-in-the-Hills. As soon as the couple moved to the corner of County Road 48 and Bloomfield Avenue, they set the plans in motion for what is now Blue Bayou Farms and Produce Market.

"The land used to be home to an orange grove, and we decided to bulldoze them and plant blueberries," says Amanda. "We added a wholesale greenhouse, then the produce stand, and then a retail garden greenhouse in which we grow chemical-free herbs. We added a commercial kitchen where we bake pies and our blueberry-orange bread.

"Our most popular pies are the blueberry, ABC [apple, blueberry, and cranberry], and our tomato-leek. My mom bakes depending on what she's in the mood for or what's in season," says Amanda. The kitchen also allows the McCormacks to package their own marmalades, fruit butters, and a sweet-and-spicy chow chow.

"Doug is a fifth-generation farmer. His dad really got him going as a young man," says Amanda, who is a nurse. "Before I met Doug, I really didn't know much about farming. Now I love it, and we've gotten our daughters and my parents very involved as well. It's nice to be with my family and socialize with the customers. There are always new and interesting people discovering the farm."

For Doug, the lifestyle of a family farm is heaven: "Doing what I love, with the people that I love—what else could I ask for?"

BLUEBERRY PIE

At Blue Bayou Farms, customers come for the produce and the freshly baked pies from the farmhouse kitchen next to the open-air market. This recipe calls for fresh fruit, but thawed and well-drained frozen berries will work just fine.

SERVES 8 TO 10

2 rolls refrigerated pie dough
¾ cup sugar
½ cup all-purpose flour
½ teaspoon cinnamon

5 cups fresh blueberries
1 tablespoon fresh lemon juice
1 tablespoon unsalted butter
1 egg, beaten
1 tablespoon water or cream

1 Line a 9-inch pie pan with one pie dough circle; set aside.

2 Combine sugar, flour, and cinnamon in a medium bowl. Add blueberries and stir gently. Carefully spoon blueberry mixture into piecrust. Sprinkle with lemon juice and dot with butter.

3 Add the second pie dough circle as a top crust, pinching edges with a fork or fingers to seal. Cut 3 slits in the top to let steam vent while pie bakes.

4 Combine beaten egg with water or cream. Brush on top crust, being careful not to leave pools of the mixture. Refrigerate pie 30 minutes.

5 Preheat oven to 400°F.

6 Bake 20 minutes. Reduce oven temperature to 350°F and bake 35 to 45 minutes more, or until crust is deep golden brown and juices are bubbly and thick. If pie's edges start to brown, cover the edges with nonstick foil.

7 Cool on wire rack for at least 2 hours before cutting.

Gracie, left, and Emily McCormack show off a blueberry pie they helped make at Blue Bayou Farms

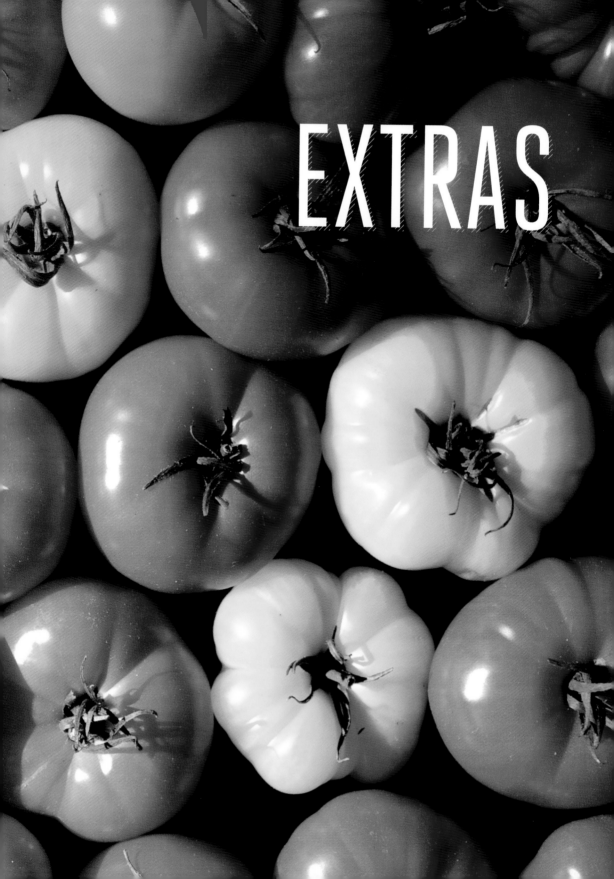

EXTRAS

GREEN FLAMINGO ORGANICS

OAK HILL

Started by New Smyrna Beach natives Liz Dannemiller and Mary Hathaway, Green Flamingo Farm supplies consumers and restaurants along Florida's Atlantic Coast with pasture-raised poultry, eggs, and produce.

"We are beyond organic," says Mary, who studied anthropology at Florida State University. She went on a research trip to Ecuador but ended up working on small farms there instead. Liz honed her skills on farms in Oregon, and in 2009, Liz and Mary began a small CSA at the two-acre farm in New Smyrna. Since then, membership has steadily grown. Green Flamingo's weekly newsletters keep members up to date on harvests and farm developments.

Mary and Liz are expanding their outreach in east Volusia County to get gardens planted in local schools. New projects to keep the property sustainable include improving rainwater catch, exploring alternative energy sources, and beekeeping.

"Food is such an important part of Florida culture and history," says Mary. "How it gets from the field to the table shouldn't be taken for granted. Small or large, Florida farms are making great strides to maintain sustainable environments. We want to be part of that movement for a long time to come."

WALKER CREEK PICKLED OKRA

If you do not want to go through the whole canning and sterilizing process, you can make these as refrigerator pickles and skip the water bath processing. Refrigerator pickles will keep chilled for up to a month. With the canned variety described here, it's ideal to wait 2 weeks to a month before eating.

MAKES 4 PINTS

4 small dried chilis, split in half
2 teaspoons mustard seeds, divided
12 sprigs dill
4 cloves garlic, peeled
2 pounds fresh okra, washed, stems trimmed
½ cup pickling salt
1 quart cider vinegar
3 quarts water

1 Place 1 chili, ½ teaspoon mustard seeds, 3 sprigs of dill, and 1 garlic clove in the bottom of each of 4 sterilized 1-pint-capacity canning jars. Divide the okra evenly among the 4 jars, standing pods up vertically, alternating stems up and down.

2 Bring the salt, cider vinegar, and water to a boil in a saucepan over medium heat. Pour mixture over okra in jars, leaving about ½ inch between top of liquid and lid. Seal. Process jars in a boiling water bath for 15 minutes.

WATERKIST FARM

SANFORD

Melanie Corun and Roger Worst, both former Federal Express couriers, wanted a family business where she could work at home. "Oh, my, be careful what you wish for," says Melanie with a laugh. They immersed themselves in learning the hydroponic business, and with help from the Seminole County Extension Office of the University of Florida's Institute of Food and Agricultural Sciences, the novices retrofitted a greenhouse (designed for growing indoor houseplants) for a hydroponic operation.

And they were off. In the beginning, Melanie mostly oversaw the production of their plump and flavorful heirloom and beefsteak tomatoes. "Quite frankly, the idea of selling the tomatoes was intimidating to me," Melanie says. "But we had to make some money." To expand their business to hotels and restaurants, they would drop off samples with a business card and let the tomatoes speak for themselves. At the same time, their farmers' market sales were steadily climbing.

"My husband would say, 'You have to come to the [Winter Park] farmers' market and hear what the customers are saying about our tomatoes.' Eventually, I did, and I was overwhelmed with pride," Melanie says, and she now loves the weekend experience. "Rain or shine, our customers are there. They tell us about seeing our produce on restaurant menus and how they use our products in their own kitchens. It's an amazing discovery each and every weekend."

As customers asked for more Waterkist produce, Melanie and Roger expanded their operation to include several varieties of lettuces, microgreens, peppers, and Mediterranean cucumbers. A fair amount of their harvest now makes its way to local restaurants, hotels, and some grocery stores, as far away as New York City, but the farmers' market is still the heart and soul of this family-owned business.

MELANIE'S FRESH SPAGHETTI SAUCE

This classic red sauce has multiple sweet notes from the sweet onions, peppers, and tomatoes, as well the addition of brown sugar. To peel tomatoes easily, cut an X in the bottom and submerge in boiling water for 45 seconds.

MAKES 2 QUARTS

½ cup olive oil
4 medium sweet onions, chopped
1 yellow bell pepper, chopped
1 teaspoon freshly ground black pepper
12 cups peeled, chopped fresh tomatoes
1 cup chopped fresh oregano

½ cup chopped fresh basil
4 teaspoons coarse salt, or to taste
2 bay leaves
1 garlic clove, minced
2 (6-ounce) cans tomato paste
2 tablespoons packed light brown sugar

1 Heat olive oil in a large stockpot over medium-high heat. Sauté onions, yellow pepper, and black pepper until the vegetables are tender, about 2 minutes. Add tomatoes, oregano, basil, salt, bay leaves, and garlic.

2 Lower heat and simmer 2 hours, stirring occasionally. Whisk in tomato paste and brown sugar and simmer 1 hour longer. Remove bay leaves before serving.

GREEN CAY PRODUCE FARMING RESEARCH SYSTEMS, INC. *FL*

BOYNTON BEACH

"When I started farming in the 1970s, it was still a rare career choice for a woman," says Dr. Nancy Roe, farmer extraordinaire with Green Cay Produce Farming Research Systems, Inc., in Boynton Beach. "No one in my family ever told me I couldn't, and as a child I was in the garden with my grandfather all the time."

Nancy did her dissertation research for a PhD in horticulture from the University of Florida at Green Cay, a 300-acre family-owned vegetable farm. When the family sold most of the land to Palm Beach County for the Green Cay Wetlands and Nature Center, they offered Nancy and her husband, Charlie, ten acres to farm and continue vegetable research. Today, their beautiful produce is sold through a successful CSA and to top-tier restaurants in the area.

"I jumped at the chance to make a third of what I was making to become a farmer," Nancy says with a laugh. But the small-farm, locally grown flavor is important, and there are no plans to expand. "I don't want to lose the connection with our customers," Nancy says.

Tomatoes are their signature crop, followed by broccoli and corn. Greens in the summer, squashes in summer and winter, herbs, root crops—"We're always trying new things."

LIBBY'S BARBECUE SAUCE

"This is an old recipe of my mother's," says Nancy. "It's very different from modern barbecue sauces, not thick or smooth, and you can actually identify the vegetables and whole spices in it. We used it for many dishes—my favorite was 'ham barbecues.' Popular in the Pittsburgh area where I grew up, the sandwiches were made with finely sliced 'chipped ham.'"

MAKES 1 QUART

4 large tomatoes, peeled and chopped
2 large onions, peeled and chopped
4 stalks celery, chopped
1 green pepper, chopped
1 small hot pepper, chopped
1 cup sugar
1 tablespoon salt
1½ teaspoons pickling spices
¼ teaspoon cinnamon

Combine tomatoes, onions, celery, green pepper, hot pepper, sugar, salt, pickling spices, and cinnamon in a heavy pot over medium heat. Bring to a boil and reduce heat to simmer. Cook uncovered, stirring frequently, 2 hours.

CHEF TOM GRAY

BISTRO AIX, JACKSONVILLE

In 1999, Tom Gray moved from Napa Valley to his hometown of Jacksonville to open Bistro AIX, a stylish, modern Mediterranean restaurant. "I came back to Florida thinking I was coming to a region where there would be a lot of easily accessible ingredients from farms," Tom says, "but at the time, that wasn't the case."

Then Tom met Denise Francis of Twinn Bridges Farm in nearby Macclenny, a meeting that proved advantageous for both chef and farmer. "Coming from California, where we had access to fresh produce grown by small farms, all within just a few miles of our home, I was really excited to form a similar relationship with a farmer in Florida," he says. "We started experimenting together, growing different things to see what flourished. So Denise got to try new things, and then I got to cook them."

Tom, who has twice been a James Beard nominee, has made a name for himself in Jacksonville cooking Mediterranean and French food (the restaurant is named for the Provençal town Aix-en-Provence). Many of the ingredients Tom uses come from local farms, including grass-fed ground beef, heritage-breed pork belly, and eggs from Twinn Bridges that he uses in the house-made pasta dough. "We've been working with local farms for more than ten years now," he says. "For us it's not a new fad. It's not a new trend. It's our lifestyle."

CHARRED-TOMATO VINAIGRETTE

Chef Tom serves this vinaigrette alongside crab cakes made with Florida blue crab. It's also delicious as a garnish for seared scallops or shrimp.

MAKES 1½ CUPS

4 ripe tomatoes, cored and halved
1 teaspoon coarse salt, divided
4 tablespoons extra virgin olive oil, divided
2 tablespoons chopped fresh thyme, divided
1 tablespoon minced garlic
½ teaspoon freshly ground black pepper, divided
1 tablespoon red wine vinegar

1 Gently squeeze tomato halves to remove seeds. Set tomatoes, cut side up, in a shallow dish and sprinkle with ½ teaspoon salt.

2 Whisk together 2 tablespoons olive oil, 1 tablespoon thyme, garlic, and ¼ teaspoon pepper in a small bowl. Spoon marinade into tomatoes. Cover and refrigerate at least 3 hours and up to overnight.

3 Place tomatoes, cut side up, on a hot outdoor or indoor grill. Allow skin to blister, then flip tomatoes over and cook until tender. Pull off and discard any skin that loosens.

4 Place tomatoes in a stainless steel or glass container. Cover and cool to room temperature. Lift tomatoes out of their juices and remove any remaining skin. Save juices. Finely chop tomatoes and place them, along with any reserved juices, in a medium bowl. Add remaining ½ teaspoon salt, remaining 2 tablespoons olive oil, remaining 1 tablespoon thyme, remaining ¼ teaspoon black pepper, and vinegar.

GREEN RAILWAY ORGANIC WORKSHOP

MIAMI

On an abandoned railway track near the Miami International Airport, there's an incongruous swath of green that reflects the transformation of an industrial warehouse district into farm space. Started in 2007, Green Railway Organic Workshop, or G.R.O.W., is a grassroots, non-profit urban farm that supports itself by growing herbs on three acres and selling them to top-tier chefs and to Rock Garden Warehouse, a wholesale distributor next door to the garden that is owned by G.R.O.W. founder, Charlie Coiner. Everything in the garden is grown in boxes, not the ground, to avoid contamination from prior industrial use.

"G.R.O.W.'s mission is to beautify and create a green space, but it's also to educate students of all ages about growing edible plants," says Thi Squire, education director. Busloads of students from area schools arrive almost daily to plant, harvest, and then make lunch using the herbs. G.R.O.W. also works with organizations to provide therapeutic learning experiences for children and adults with hardships and disabilities.

"Generations have lost the skill to cook," says Thi. When it's time for lunch, the students gather around a big table right next to the garden and watch as Thi magically transform herbs and a handful of other ingredients into something fresh and delicious.

"We're hoping to create a new generation who understands where their food comes from," Thi says.

G.R.O.W. GODDESS DRESSING

Thi makes this simple dressing with whatever herbs are ready to harvest—she lets the youngsters pick the herbs, then makes the dressing on the spot and serves with fresh veggies. Delicious with everything from fresh vegetables to hot fritters and chilled cooked shrimp.

SERVES 4

¼ cup mayonnaise
¼ cup sour cream or plain yogurt
¼ teaspoon cayenne pepper
Juice of ½ lemon
½ cup favorite assorted herbs, such as chives, chervil, mint, parsley
Coarse salt and freshly ground black pepper, to taste

Place mayonnaise, sour cream or yogurt, cayenne pepper, lemon, herbs, salt, and pepper in a blender and blend until smooth.

Facing: Thi Squire

CHEF NORMAN VAN AKEN

NORMAN'S, ORLANDO

Chef Norman Van Aken grew up in midwestern farm country in the 1950s and 1960s, with a Girl Scout leader mom who was always canning, making homemade jams, and preserving. "We shopped in a shed by the side of the road in the summertime," says Norman. "This was my introduction to cuisine."

At twenty-one, he hitchhiked to Key West and "fell in love with this bohemian, artistic place," he recalls. "My natural instinct from midwestern America was to be around working-class people—but they worked on boats instead of tractors."

The self-taught chef worked in kitchens from Illinois to Florida to refine his skills, and by 1985, he was cooking at Louie's Backyard in Key West, where his culinary star began to rise. Captivated by exotic tropical fruits and Caribbean flavors, Norman blended Latin, Caribbean, Asian, African, and American cuisines, earning the title of founding father of New World Cuisine, a style of cooking that celebrates America's ethnicity.

His global approach to cooking brought meteoric success, including the James Beard Award in 1997 for Best Chef in the Southeast, and acclaim from the *New York Times* and *Gourmet* magazine for his Miami restaurant, Norman's of Coral Gables. (The Coral Gables restaurant has closed, but he still oversees Norman's at the Ritz-Carlton Grande Lakes in Orlando.)

And now the times, he says, are changing. Norman credits his son, Justin Van Aken, part of the next generation of young chefs, with taking his thinking full circle. "Justin challenges me to think back to the original ideas of how to cook, how to think about food . . . how to be more in sync with the farm-to-table simplicity, to focus on Florida's distinct cuisine."

It's been nearly two decades since Norman started sourcing from South Florida growers, creating haute cuisine from everything from collards to passion fruit. "It's always been natural to source locally, but now I have a deeper appreciation for what Florida offers," Norman says. "Justin's generation has a clear understanding of the finiteness of sources in a way we did not."

TROPICAL CHUTNEY

Norman recommends serving this chutney with ham, grilled chicken, or pork chops. Lychees, used often in Asian cooking, are a sweet, fragrant tropical fruit that thrives in the sultry climate of South Florida.

MAKES 4 CUPS

½ cup sugar
1 small red onion, diced medium
1 mango, peeled, seeded, diced medium
½ papaya or pineapple, peeled, diced medium (about 1 cup)
1 Granny Smith apple, peeled and diced medium
1 Asian pear, diced medium
1 tablespoon Chinese five-spice powder
Course salt and freshly ground black pepper, to taste
1 cup apple cider vinegar
1 stalk lemongrass, chopped
1 star anise
10 lychees, cleaned and roughly chopped

1 Mix together sugar, onion, mango, papaya or pineapple, apple, Asian pear, and five-spice powder. Season to taste with salt and pepper. Set aside.

2 Stir together vinegar, lemongrass, and star anise in a saucepan over medium heat. Bring to a boil, reduce heat, and cook until liquid is reduced to ¾ cup. Remove from heat and strain.

3 Combine fruit mixture with strained juices in a large heavy saucepan over medium heat. Cook about 30 minutes, then strain juices into another saucepan.

4 Bring juices to a boil, reduce heat, and cook until reduced until almost a syrup consistency. Combine syrup with fruit.

5 Add lychees to chutney and season to taste with salt and pepper.

HATCHER MANGO HILL

LANTANA

In the early 1940s in Lantana, pioneer citrus grower John Hatcher set out to make a better mango. And he did, officially registering the sweet, remarkably nonfibrous variety under the family name.

Once John realized the delectable quality of the fruit, he planted a four-acre mango orchard that he proudly named Hatcher Mango Hill. And though there may be backyard Hatcher trees in addition to the Lantana grove, the Hatcher has remained relatively unknown among commercial growers and is on the Slow Food USA Ark of Taste as a food in danger of extinction. The property, too, is at high risk because of encroaching development; the gravel entrance road is now just off Interstate 95.

John's son, Richard, and his wife, Marilynn, inherited Hatcher Mango Hill, where the distinctive Hatcher still is the star of the grove. The pale green to yellow fruit with a reddish-orange blush can weigh more than two pounds. And though Richard passed away in 2006, Marilynn continues the story with internet orders for multiple varieties of mango, picked fresh every morning, seven days a week in the summertime, with the Hatcher ready for shipping in July and August. After the mango season is finished, specially grafted trees are for sale—a way to keep the sweet Hatcher living.

MANGO MAGIC PRESERVES

Marilynn wrote her own cookbook, *Hatcher's Mango Thrills*, and this is her recipe. "Use your own good taste and good sense when preserving any fruit," says Marilynn. "They can vary in ripeness, water content, sweetness, and variety."

MAKES 6 (8-OUNCE) JARS

8 cups mangos, peeled, pitted, sliced
2 cups sugar
2 tablespoon Key lime juice

1 Toss mango slices with sugar in a large bowl and let stand at room temperature for 2 to 3 hours, stirring occasionally.

2 Sterilize 6 (8-ounce) canning jars and lids according to manufacturer's instructions. Heat water in a hot water canner.

3 Pour mango slices and juice in a colander over a heavy shallow saucepan; drain for 15 minutes, then set fruit aside in a bowl.

4 Place saucepan of juice over high heat and add Key lime juice; boil about 10 minutes, or until liquid thickens to a syrup. Stir in mango slices and any additional juice. Cook over high heat until mangos are golden and caramelized around edges, stirring occasionally.

5 Heat water in a hot water canner. Quickly ladle mango mixture into sterilized jars, filling to within ¼ inch of the top. Wipe jar rims clean, cover with flat lids, and screw on bands tightly.

6 Place jars in rack and slowly lower rack into canner. The water should cover jars completely and should be hot but not boiling. Bring water to a boil and process 5 minutes.

7 Remove jars from hot water bath and let cool.

FOX HOLLOW VINEYARD

SNEADS

Every time Susan Howell-Paul considered her sprawling front yard, she had the urge to grow something that would be sustainable and edible, but also something that didn't require full-time attention. "I have a day job," Susan says with a smile, "so I needed something that wouldn't create too much additional work." She tossed around several possibilities before landing on the large, thick-skinned grapes called muscadines.

Muscadine grapevines don't require constant attention, and they grow well in North Florida's hot, humid summers and relatively cool winters. Susan says it seemed like the natural choice. Along with the vines are two pomegranate trees and two olive trees, all of which are prolific in the warm months.

Starting August 1 each year, Fox Hollow is open for business. Most of the grapes are sold through U-pick, and Susan gathers what remains and sells them at local markets. She doesn't use any sprays on the grapes or the vines, and she encourages wildlife like deer ("they keep the low-hanging grapes from rotting on the ground") and bluebirds to live freely among the vines. "I just try to fit in and share with nature."

MUSCADINE-PEPPER JELLY

Two of the four varieties of muscadines Susan grows are perfect for jelly, which she serves over cream cheese or chèvre with crusty baguette rounds and crackers. Leave the seeds in the jalapeño, if desired, for a spicier jelly. Crushed red pepper flakes can also be added to increase spiciness. Use a juicer or blender to make the muscadine juice—just be sure to strain out seeds and skin.

MAKES 6 (8-OUNCE) JARS

2½ cups finely chopped red bell pepper
¼ cup finely chopped green bell pepper
¼ cup seeded and finely chopped jalapeño
    pepper
1½ cups muscadine juice
½ cup apple cider vinegar
2 (1.75 ounce) packages powdered pectin
5 cups sugar
1 teaspoon butter (optional; helps to cut down on
    foam during cooking process)

1 Sterilize 6 (8-ounce) canning jars and lids according to manufacturer's instructions. Heat water in a hot water canner.

2 Place all peppers in a large saucepan over high heat. Stir in muscadine juice, vinegar, and pectin. Bring mixture to a full rolling boil, stirring constantly. Quickly stir in sugar and butter, if using. Return to rolling boil and boil exactly 2 minutes, stirring constantly. Remove from heat and skim off any foam.

3 Quickly ladle jelly into sterilized jars, filling to within ¼ inch of the top. Wipe jar rims clean, cover with flat lids, and screw on bands tightly.

4 Place jars in rack and slowly lower rack into canner. The water should cover jars completely and should be hot but not boiling. Bring water to a boil and process 5 minutes.

5 Remove jars from hot water bath and let cool.

STRUTHERS' HONEY

LAKE WALES

As you are heading east on U.S. Highway 60, a white building breaks the monotony of the flat grazing land dotted with cattle and egrets. Welcome to Struthers' Honey in Hesperides, a hamlet so small that it almost merges into greater Lake Wales. Struthers' has been selling honey ("A Pound or A Carload") since 1935.

Inside the small store, the walls are covered with newspaper clippings, family photos, and honey information. The golden elixir is bottled in an assortment of containers and displayed in rows on shelves. Price tags are clearly placed on each bottle, but don't wait for an attendant to greet you. Whoever is working that day is tending to the honey in the packinghouse out back. The honor system has been in play here since 1935, and Alden and Lotta Kay Struthers have no intention of changing things now.

"In the beginning, customers put their money in a coffee can," Lotta Kay says. "Today, we have a large bench with a slot for money in the center. It works for us and it's become part of the Struthers' history." All of the honey comes from local bees. Word of mouth has served the Struthers family well, and the family still sees no need for a website or advertising. "You don't see a lot of people standing in line to be beekeepers," Lotta Kay says. "It's hard work. We plan to stay with it for as long as we can. Hopefully, the legacy will continue."

HONEY-ORANGE CREAM

Use this thick cream to bind fresh fruit salads or ambrosia mixtures, or dollop on warm waffles or pancakes.

MAKES 1 CUP

½ cup heavy whipping cream
2 tablespoons orange-blossom honey
1 teaspoon orange zest

Beat whipping cream until it is just fluffy. Fold in honey and continue beating until stiff peaks form. Fold in orange zest.

MENU SUGGESTIONS

SPRING DINNER ALFRESCO

Summer Fruit Salad with Fresh Mint Dressing

Carambola Honey-Glazed Chicken

Hua Moa Tostones

Minorcan Black Beans

Cantaloupe Sherbet

Siesta Key Lime Martini

FOURTH OF JULY BACKYARD BARBECUE

Cool Gazpacho with Harissa-Grilled
Wild-Caught American White Shrimp

Dry-Rubbed Baby Back Ribs and
Libby's Barbecue Sauce

Southern Fried Corn

Tomato-Papaya Salad

Watermelon-Rose Ice Pops or
Fresh Blackberry Milkshakes

Fresh Passion Fruit Juice

BEACH EATS

Mahi Mahi and Longan Ceviche

Pulled Pork Banh-Mi

Cilantro-Lime Kohl Slaw

Rosemary-Pecan Shortbread Cookies

Spicy Strawberry Margarita

SOUTHERN SUMMER BRUNCH BUFFET

Callaloo and Okra Summer Quiche

Crab Cakes with Charred-Tomato Vinaigrette

Warm Buttermilk Biscuits with Mango Magic
Preserves and Muscadine-Pepper Jelly

Chilled Haricots Verts with Crème Fraîche
Vinaigrette and Hazelnuts

Smoky Gouda Grits

Cinnamon Buns

Pecan Pralines with Dark Chocolate
and Sel Gris

Peace River Caipiroska

FALL TAILGATE

Cajun-Style Boiled Peanuts

Walker Creek Pickled Okra

Margie's Chunky Guacamole and Chips

Deep Creek Lamb Burgers

Baked Penne with Four Cheeses

Classic Key Lime Pie

Florida Garden Sangria

HOLIDAYS FLORIDA-STYLE

Creamy Wild Mushroom Soup

Brined and Herb Butter–Basted Turkey

Spicy-Sweet Kale

Purple Cabbage and Goat Cheese Sauté

Mushroom Medley Potato Cakes

Chocolate Chestnut Torte with Ganache Glaze

EASY WINTER SUPPER

Lamb and Kale Stew

Grilled Cheese with Fig Jam and Escarole

Tupelo Honey Baklava Rolls

Umatilla Smash

WHERE TO FIND THE FARMS, CHEFS, AND ARTISANS

FARMS

We've denoted with a star farms that are open to the public or offer tours or special events that are booked in advance. Keep in mind that farms also are often the farmers' home. Make sure to call ahead.

NORTH FLORIDA

Chestnut Hill Tree Farm* 236
15105 NW 94th Ave.
Alachua, FL 32615
386-462-2820 or
800-669-2067
www.chestnuthilltreefarm.com

Down to Earth Farm 84
Jacksonville, FL
904-525-3309

Dragonfly Fields 36
DeFuniak Springs, FL
850-259-3739

Fox Hollow Vineyard* 280
8160 Renegade Pass
Sneads, FL 32460
850-593-2202

Full Earth Farm 172
Quincy, FL
850-567-1493
fullearthfarm@gmail.com

Green Cedars Farm* 135
9280 Gibson Rd.
Molino, FL 32577
850-698-0107
www.greencedarsfarm.com

Green Gate Olive Grove* 238
Jackson County, FL
850-763-6355
www.greengateolivegrove.com

Hammock Hollow 211
Island Grove, FL

Heirloom Country Farms 138
Archer, FL
352-337-2541
www.heirloomcountryfarms.
bravehost.com

Holland Farms* 34
2055 Homer Holland Rd.
Milton, FL 32570
850-675-6876

Maggie's Herb Farm* 222
11400 County Rd. 13
St. Augustine, FL 32092
www.maggiesherbfarm.com

Ocheesee Creamery* 208
28367 NE State Rd. 69
Grand Ridge, FL 32442
850-674-8620

Orchard Pond Organics* 226
500 Orchard Pond Rd.
Tallahassee, FL 32312
850-591-5766
www.orchardpondorganics.com

Paisley Pecan Company 214
Paisley, FL
352-669-9627
www.paisleypecanfarms.com

Smiley Apiaries* 216
161 Bozeman Circle
Wewahitchka, FL 32465
www.floridatupelohoney.com

Smith Family Farm* 92
9365 Hastings Blvd.
Hastings, FL 32145
904-392-7958
www.smithfamilyproduce.com

Superganic Farms 160
Pensacola, FL
850-434-5679
www.superganicfarms.com

Swallowtail CSA* 169
27431 N. County Rd. 1491
Alachua, FL 32615
352-327-1175
www.swallowtailcsa.com

Terk's Acres* 46
3000 Joe Ashton Rd.
St. Augustine, FL 32092
904-824-4871
www.terksacres.com

Turkey Hill Farm 102
Tallahassee, FL
850-216-4024

Twin Oaks Farm 112
Bonifay, FL
850-547-5636
www.twinoaksfarm.net

Wynn Heritage Farms* 203
668 SW Gabriella Way
Madison, FL 32340
850-973-2729
www.wynnheritagefarms.com

CENTRAL FLORIDA

B&W Quality Growers 74
Fellsmere, FL
772-571-0800
www.bwqualitygrowers.com

Blue Bayou Farms* 254
26921 Bloomfield Ave.
Yalaha, FL 34737
352-324-4069
www.bluebayoufarms.com

Crazy Hart Ranch 108
Fellsmere, FL
772-913-0036
www.crazyhartranch.com

Dakin Dairy Farms* 190
30771 Betts Rd.
Myakka City, FL 34251
941-322-2802
www.dakindairyfarms.com

Deep Creek Ranch 136
DeLeon Springs, FL
386-216-2442
www.deepcreekranch.us

Desoto Lakes Organics &
Jessica's Farm Stand* 158
4180 47th St.
Sarasota, FL 34235
941-993-2064
www.jessicasorganicfarm.com

Duda Farm Fresh Foods 186
Oviedo, FL
407-365-2111
www.dudafresh.com

Favorite Farms, Inc.* 20
10070 McIntosh Rd.
Dover, FL 33527
813-986-3949
www.favoritefarms.net

Florida's Natural Growers* 146
20205 N. U.S. Highway 27
Lake Wales, FL 33853
888-657-6600
www.floridasnatural.com

Green Flamingo Organics* 260
398 N. Putnam Grove Rd.
Oak Hill, FL 32759
386-478-9923
www.greenflamingoorganics.
com

Lake Meadow Naturals* 218
10000 Mark Adam Rd.
Ocoee, FL 34761
www.lakemeadownaturals.net

Lightsey Cattle Co. 128
Lake Wales, FL

Long & Scott Farms* 77
PO Box 1228
Zellwood, FL 32798
352-383-6900
www.longandscottfarms.com

Mark's U-Pick Blueberries* 52
18900 County Rd. 561
Clermont, FL 34715
352-394-2135
www.marksblueberries.com

Monterey Mushrooms 194
Zellwood, FL
407-905-4000
www.montereymushrooms.com

Neat and Sweet Farms 204
Lakeland, FL
863-816-1444

Palmetto Creek Farms 145
Avon Park, FL
863-449-0006
www.bestpork.us

Parkesdale Farms
and Market* 18
3702 W. Baker St.
Plant City, FL 33563
813-754-2704 or 888-311-1701

Pasture Prime
Family Farm* 142
4141 SE 180th St.
Summerfield, FL 34491
352-266-9504
www.pastureprimewagyu.com

Petteway Citrus & Cattle 132
Zolfo Springs, FL
863-773-2303
www.citrusandcattle.com

Pure Produce* 149
8875 Fleming Grant Road
Micco, FL 32976
772-664-3657
www.pureproduce.com

Shady Acres
Strawberry Farm* 244
3420 Gallagher Rd.
Dover, FL 33527
813-659-0222

Struthers' Honey* 283
8024 Rose Terrace
Lake Wales, FL 33898

3 Boys Farm 50
Ruskin, FL
813-645-5445
www.3boysfarm.com

Tropical Blossom
Honey Co.* 221
106 N. Ridgewood Ave.
Edgewater, FL 32132
386-428-9027
www.tropicalbeehoney.com

Uncle Matt's Organic 106
Clermont, FL
352-394-8737
www.unclematts.com

Waterkist Farm 264
Sanford, FL

Wishnatzki Farms 60
Plant City, FL
813-752-5111
www.wishfarms.com

Worden Farm* 69
34900 Bermont Rd.
Punta Gorda, FL 33982
941-637-4874
www.wordenfarm.com

SOUTH FLORIDA
Alger Farms 178
Homestead, FL
305-247-4334
www.algerfarms.com

Bee Heaven Farm 41
Redland, FL
305-247-8650
www.pikarco.com

Burr's Berry Farm* 234
12741 SW 216th St.
Miami, FL 33170
305-251-0145
www.burrsberryfarm.com

C&B Farms, Inc. 86
Hendry County, FL
863-983-8269

D&D Farms U-Pick* 96
5059 SW Citrus Blvd.
Palm City, FL 34990
772-240-8138
www.danddfarms.com

Erickson Farm* 228
13646 U.S. Highway 441
Canal Point, FL 33438
561-924-7714
www.ericksonfarm.com

Fairchild Farm* 62
14885 SW 248th St.
Homestead, FL 33032
305-258-0464
www.fairchildgarden.org

Gaby's Farm 10
Homestead, FL
305-246-7702
www.gabysfarm.com

Going Bananas* 230
24401 SW 197th Ave.
Homestead, FL 33031
305-247-0397
www.going-bananas.com

Green Cay Produce 267
Boynton Beach, FL
561-638-2755
www.veggies4u.com

Green Railway Organic
Workshop* 272
2950 Northwest 74th Ave.
Miami, FL 33122
305-477-8833
www.rockgardenherbs.com

Hatcher Mango Hill 277
Lantana, FL
561-588-6098
www.hatchermangohill.com

Knaus Berry Farm* 252
15980 SW 248th St.
Homestead, FL 33031
305-247-0668
www.knausberryfarm.com

Larson Dairy, Inc. 240
Okeechobee, FL
863-763-7330

Little River Market Garden 88
Miami, FL
www.littlerivercsa.com

Paradise Farms* 54
1801 SW 320th St.
Homestead, FL 33030
305-248-4181
www.paradisefarms.net

Pine Island Botanicals 49
Bokeelia, FL
239-283-8817
www.pineislandbotanicals.com

Possum Trot Tropical Fruit
Nursery* 104
14955 SW 214th St.
Miami, FL 33187
305-235-1768

Robert Is Here* 246
19200 SW 344th St.
Homestead, FL 33034
305-246-1592
www.robertishere.com

Roth Farms 115
Belle Glade, FL
561-993-3037
www.rothfarms.com

Satur Farms 15
Palm Beach County, FL
631-734-4219
www.saturfarms.com

Swank Specialty
Produce* 95
14311 North Rd.
Loxahatchee, FL 33470
561-202-5648
www.swankfarms.com

Teena's Pride* 58
20025 SW 270th St.
Homestead, FL 33031
305-216-2336
www.teenaspride.com

Varri Green Farm* 30
12847 SE Highway 441
Okeechobee, FL 34974
863-357-2747
www.varrigreenfarm.com

CHEFS AND ARTISANS

NORTH FLORIDA

Chef Tom Gray 270
Bistro AIX
1440 San Marco Blvd.
Jacksonville, FL 32207
904-398-1949

Chef David Gwynn 70
Cypress Restaurant
320 E. Tennessee St.
Tallahassee, FL 32301
850-513-1100

Chefs Jonathan Insetta and Brian Siebenschuh 154
Restaurant Orsay
3630 Park St.
Jacksonville, FL 32205
904-381-0909

Craig and Barbie Raynor 188
Taste of Old St. Augustine
St. Augustine, FL
904-829-1109
info@tasteofstaugustine.com

Chef Jim Shirley 120
The Great Southern Café
83 Center Ave.
Seaside, FL 32459
850-231-7327
www.thegreatsoutherncafe.com

CENTRAL FLORIDA

Chef Kevin Fonzo 124
K Restaurant & Wine Bar
1710 Edgewater Dr.
Orlando, FL 32804
407-872-2332
www.kwinebar.com

Chef Scott Hunnel 38
Victoria & Albert's
Disney's Grand Floridian
Resort & Spa
4401 Floridian Way
Lake Buena Vista, FL
32830-8416
407-939-3862
www.victoria-alberts.com

Chef Brandon
McGlamery 212
Luma on Park
290 S. Park Ave.
Winter Park, FL 32789
407-599-4111
www.lumaonpark.com

Chefs Julie and James
Petrakis 98
The Ravenous Pig
1234 N. Orange Ave.
Winter Park, FL 32789
407-628-2333
www.theravenouspig.com

Chef Kathleen Blake 293
The Rusty Spoon
55 W. Church St.
Orlando, FL 32801
407-401-8811
www.therustyspoon.com

Chef Hari Pulapaka 117
Cress
103 W. Indiana Ave.
DeLand, FL 32720
386-734-3740
www.cressrestaurant.com

Chefs Henry and Michele
Salgado 42
Spanish River Grill
737 E. Third Ave.
New Smyrna Beach, FL 32169
386-424-6991
www.thespanishrivergrill.com

Chef Norman Van Aken 274
Norman's
The Ritz-Carlton Orlando,
Grande Lakes
4012 Central Florida Parkway
Orlando, FL 32737
407-393-4333
www.normans.com

Chef Roy Yamaguchi 51
Roy's Restaurant
Various Florida locations
www.roysrestaurant.com

Palm Ridge Reserve 23
Umatilla, FL
352-455-7232
www.palmridgereserve.com

Drum Circle Distilling 15
Sarasota, FL
www.drumcircledistilling.com

SOUTH FLORIDA
Chef Michelle Bernstein 250
Michy's
6927 Biscayne Blvd.
Miami, FL 33138
305-759-2001
www.michysmiami.com

Chef Paula DaSilva 162
1500 Degrees at the Eden Roc
4525 Collins Ave.
Miami Beach, FL
305-674-5594

Chef Dean Max 64
3030 Ocean Restaurant
Marriott's Harbor Beach Resort
& Spa
3030 Holiday Dr.
Ft. Lauderdale, FL 33316
954-765-3030
www.3030ocean.com

Redland Mediterranean
Organics 177
Miami, FL
305-562-3202
www.hanisorganics.com

Chef Michael Schwartz 166
Michael's Genuine Food & Drink
130 Northeast 40th St.
Miami, FL 33137
305-573-5550
www.michaelsgenuine.com

4 Orange Premium Vodka 12
Palm Beach Gardens, FL
www.4orangevodka.com

RECIPES AT A GLANCE

FLORIDA'S UNUSUAL INGREDIENTS

While oranges and grapefruits are familiar tastes, Florida has its share of unusual fruits and vegetables, thanks to South Florida's subtropical climate and Central Florida's temperate zones. Beautiful produce with lovely fragrances fills a kitchen with pleasing aromas. Here are some of the most unusual.

CALLALOO
This Caribbean transplant is the large leaf of the taro root; similar in taste and texture to spinach, with a slightly bitter edge.

CARAMBOLA
Also known as star fruit because of the shape of the fruit when sliced; carambola has a crisp texture and lightly sweet flavor with a thin, edible skin.

ESCAROLE
Slightly bitter greens with broad, pale green leaves with frilly tips.

FLORIDA AVOCADO
Florida was the first state to grow avocados, though most now come from California. The Florida fruit dwarfs its West Coast cousins in size and is distinguished by a smooth, green, shiny exterior.

GUAVA
This large, round green fruit has a bright pink interior; it is very aromatic with a sweet, decidedly tropical flavor.

HABANERO
An intense firecracker of a pepper, the small, paper lantern–shaped chili develops vibrant orange and red hues as it matures.

HUA MOA
This banana-plantain hybrid has a roundish shape. It hails from Polynesia, but found its way to South Florida in 1960. Farmers in South Florida call it "plátano hawaiano."

KEY LIMES
Small and round, Key limes are light yellow-green in color. They have a higher acidity than Persian limes and a distinctive aroma.

KOHLRABI

With a round, pale green bulb, kohlrabi resembles a turnip with stems and leaves protruding from the bulb. Flavor is turnip-like yet mild. The leaves are edible.

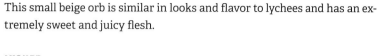

LONGAN

This small beige orb is similar in looks and flavor to lychees and has an extremely sweet and juicy flesh.

LYCHEE

This small, round fruit grows with a thick, bumpy skin. Similar in looks and flavor to longans, the pulp is a translucent milky white with a crisp, juicy texture and a sweet, roselike flavor.

MUSCADINE

To the uninitiated, a muscadine is just a grape on steroids. The table tennis ball–sized grape has a dusky skin, a pleasant, musky aroma, and sweet flesh.

PAPAYA

This large, oblong fruit isn't much to look at from the outside, but the flesh inside is a beautiful sunset orange hue and has a lightly sweet flavor.

PASSION FRUIT

This fruit has a jellylike pulp that is yellowish-orange to orange with a very aromatic, sweet, floral flavor. The black seeds are edible.

SWAMP CABBAGE

This is the tender heart of the cabbage palm, which grows wild and is protected from indiscriminate cutting as Florida's official state tree. It can be legally harvested only on private land.

TATSOI

Asian greens that are sometimes called rosette bok choy. With dark green leaves that are slightly curved, the taste is somewhat spicy.

TUPELO HONEY

A somewhat rare premium honey produced in Northwest Florida from the nectar of the tupelo gum tree. The flavor is mild and delicate. The honey never crystallizes because of its low glucose level.

ACKNOWLEDGMENTS

Writing this book has been a reflective experience, with many hours on the road, in our kitchens, and at our desks. We offer tremendous thanks to our families for their boundless support, and to the wonderful farmers who took the time from their busy days to walk us through the fields or sit around a table and tell us their stories.

We are ever so grateful to our trusted friends who tested and retested every recipe in this book: Leena Buchy, Julie Edwards, Mary-Frances Emmons, Valerie Hart, Jen Perry, Sarah Pitcock, and Lytle Wurtzel. Your thoughtful input truly makes the recipes shine. And thank you to Anne-Marie Denicole for contributing her creative recipes.

Thanks to Gary Bogdon for glorious photos that help to tell the story, and to our gifted designer, Jason Farmand, who teamed up to bring the pages to life. And to Morgan Claytor from Orlando's Hatchet Design for her stylish illustrations, which give the book even more personality.

To Erickson Farm, Inc., in Canal Point, Florida, for beautiful mangos for the photo shoot. And to Homegrown Co-op in Orlando for sharing their bounty in photos.

To Tracy Louthain and Elisa Smith from the Beaches of South Walton and Laura Lee from Visit Pensacola for their expert advice and guidance in navigating the Panhandle.

To the Hibiscus Coffee & Guesthouse for the lovely accommodations.

To Lisa Lochridge at the Florida Fruit & Vegetable Association, the folks at the Florida Beef Council, Mick Lochridge of the Florida Dairy Farmers, and the Florida Department of Agriculture and Consumer Services.

Thanks to a cadre of volunteer proofreaders who scoured each recipe: Wesley Alden, Mary Anna Gentleman, Jennie Hess, Liam Miller, Jen Perry, Susan Whigham, Dan Wine, and Lytle Wurtzel.

Thanks to Meredith Babb at the University Press of Florida, who believed in the idea from the start. And to our wonderful editor, Michele Fiyak-Burkley, and design and production manager, Lynn Werts, for keeping the book on track. And to University Press publicist Stephanie Williams for spreading the word.

We are grateful to the *Orlando Sentinel* for allowing us to use photography from the newspaper's archive.

FROM PAM: To my husband, Steve, who designed a beautiful kitchen that we used as our photo studio, and to Katie and Will, for their love, which keeps me going. To my many fantastic friends, especially Julie Edwards and Helen Miller, who insisted on exercise breaks and coached me along the journey.

FROM KATIE: A great big thank-you to my husband, Jason, for doing all the driving and being a willing travel partner and recipe taster. To Brooke Bell at *Taste of the South* magazine and Heather Thalwitzer for their great advice. And to the friends who thoughtfully tasted the many iterations of these recipes and lent great support in the process of writing this book.

FROM HEATHER: To Spencer Pettit, my wonderful husband, who is as passionate about culinary adventures as I am. To my parents, who taught all their children to be gracious hosts.

ABOUT THE AUTHORS

Pam Brandon is managing editor of *Edible Orlando* magazine and a food columnist for OrlandoSentinel.com and the *Palm Beach Post*. She has written eleven cookbooks, including *Delicious Disney Holidays* and the 2012 Epcot International Food & Wine Festival cookbook. Pam grew up in West Virginia, where farm to table was a way of life. Her favorite taste of Florida is a toss-up: spicy hot boiled peanuts or wild-caught Gulf shrimp.

Katie Farmand claims the rare title of native Floridian. She was born and raised in the Sunshine State sipping Polar Cups and eating backyard tomatoes in February. Katie is the editor of *Edible Orlando* magazine and a freelance food writer, recipe developer, and food stylist. Her recipes have been featured in the *Palm Beach Post*, the *Orlando Sentinel*, and the *Tampa Tribune*. Her blog, TheThinChef.com, is a collection of her original recipes and photography. This is her first cookbook.

Heather McPherson is the food editor and restaurant critic for the *Orlando Sentinel* and a past president of the Association of Food Journalists. She has written two cookbooks, including *Barbecue! Great Ideas for Backyard Get-Togethers*, and has edited four others, including *The Florida Cookbook: A Lighter Look at Southern Cooking*. Heather grew up in Indiana sneaking vine-ripe cherry tomatoes from her grandmother's summer garden and helping her mother, sister, and cousins snap beans for family dinners. For her, no Florida meal is complete without local beef, sweet corn, fried okra, warm biscuits dripping with honey, and late-winter berries.

* * *

The University Press of Florida is the scholarly publishing agency for the State University System of Florida, comprising Florida A&M University, Florida Atlantic University, Florida Gulf Coast University, Florida International University, Florida State University, New College of Florida, University of Central Florida, University of Florida, University of North Florida, University of South Florida, and University of West Florida.

Heather McPherson, Katie Farmand,
and Pam Brandon

ADDITIONAL PHOTO CREDITS

All photographs not listed below are by Gary Bogdon

Courtesy of Michelle Bernstein: page 250

Courtesy of Kathleen Blake: 78

Courtesy of JR Books: 40

Stephen Brandon: 31, 55, 88, 234, 246

Elizabeth Dannemiller: 261

Courtesy of Paula DaSilva: 162

Courtesy of Duda Farm Fresh Foods: 186

Katie Farmand: 13, 85, 102–3, 112, 138, 168, 226

Courtesy of Florida Department of Agriculture and Consumer Services: 240

Courtesy of Florida Fruit & Vegetable Association: 273

Courtesy of Going Bananas: 230

Jensen Hande: 154

Courtesy of the Honey Board: 282

Ian Maguire: 11

David Manning: 72–73, 140–41, 197, 198–99, 287

Courtesy of Dean Max: 65, 67

Courtesy of the *Orlando Sentinel*: 106, 122–24, 180, 212, 280

Courtesy of Hari Pulapaka: 117

Courtesy of Henry Salgado: 42

Courtesy of Satur Farms: 171

Courtesy of Michael Schwartz: 166

Svetlana Simon: 109

Courtesy of State Archives of Florida: 185

Courtesy of Allen Susser: 24

Courtesy of 3 Boys Farm: 50

Courtesy of Tom Gray: 270

Courtesy of Norman Van Aken: 272

Courtesy of the Walt Disney Company: 38

Courtesy of www.regalpeppers.com: 188

Shelley Yates: 120

INDEX